Reflections
In
Clay

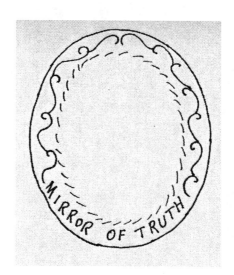

Marianne McGriffin, S. P.

ISBN: 1-4033-7535-6 (e-book)
ISBN: 1-4033-7536-4 (Paperback)

Library of Congress Control Number: 2002094528

This book is printed on acid free paper.

Printed in the United States of America
Bloomington, IN

1stBooks - rev. 02/04/03

ACKNOWLEDGEMENTS

Besides the assistance I received from numerous friends and 'computer gurus' such as Cathy Wenzel, Bill and Dennis Wolf, encouragement and nudging along by participants in programs and close friends, I wish to acknowledge the following for their contributions, permissions to publish, to quote, and to otherwise 'use' their materials.

BUCKNER, JOYCE, of Michigan City, IN. "*Genesis in Clay*," an unpublished poem written after a session of praying with clay, and sent with permission to be used 'in a book you will write some day.'

BUSER, SISTER MARTHA, OSU, Louisville, KY. My retreat director who gave me a chunk of clay and said, 'See what happens.'

BUENING, SISTER HELEN, OSB, of Mt. St. Scholastica, Atchison, KS. Sister Helen gave me written permission to use her reflections, shared during the Clay and Fire Retreat, and her reflections and art work in the article published in BENEDICTINES, 1982. References to her may be as HELEN OF ATCHISON.

COREY, TERRY, of Elkhart, IN, who gave me a word processor, coached me through beginning to use it, and set me on the path of getting things down on paper.

GUASCH, JUDITH, of Fairfield, PA, wrote '*Praying with Clay Reflections*' in a letter sent to Sister Marianne with permission to publish, June, 1999.

KEATING, THOMAS, OSCO. Quote taken from Contemplative Outreach News, Volt 13 # 1. July, 1999.

KEENE, SISTER MARY CATHERINE, S. P. who wrote 'A pot is...', a poem written for Karen Van De Walle, CSJ, Potter. Used with permission.

LILLISTON, BRENDA GLANZER. '*A Healing Deeper than Physical Pain*', published in MENNONITE MEDICAL MESSENGER, now called MENNONITE HEALTH JOURNAL. Jan./Feb./Mar. 1989, pp 7-19. This article was written while Brenda was an M. Div. student at Associated Mennonite Biblical Seminaries, Elkhart, IN. Used with permission of author and publisher.

SHALEM INSTITUTE of SPIRITUAL FORMATION, 5430, Grosvenor Lane, Bethesda, MD, 20814. Leaders, Tilden Edwards, Gerald May and Rosemary Dougherty affirmed, supported, and helped me develop confidence in the call to spiritual direction.

SMITH, JANE CORS, of Mishawaka, IN. Coworker at St. Vincent Church 1985-1988, wrote '*Transformation Mirrored in Clay*,' an account of her experience in FOCUSING and in PRAYING WITH CLAY.

TRZIL, SISTER ROSEANN, OSSF, who introduced me to the experience of guided imagery in meditation, 1980 through 1986, and whom I associate with "The Potter Woman" who sent me into the 'sea of contemplation.'

DEDICATION

I dedicate this book to all who have asked me,
"Is there a book about praying with clay?"
And to all who respond to the call to move inward,
A gift to you and to me, of the One who calls,
And who waits to be found within the inner passages
And wondrous places
You will discover in your own interior.

PROLOGUE

This book is response to a need expressed many times by many people who experienced praying with clay for the first time in my presence. Their desire to know more about this 'different' way of praying prompted their question, "Is there a book about praying with clay?" I made a promise: "I haven't found one yet, but there will be one some day."

I had looked, and continued to look for a book about praying with clay. In my long search for such books, I found several that extol the deeply spiritual intimacy of the potter with her clay, the artist with her paint, stone, words or music, but I had found none that describe the sensate/intuitive process of allowing our hands to find and shape our prayer with clay as I have developed it.

The books I did find are listed in the bibliography because I have received much inspiration from each of them and I think readers of this book may want to pursue the subject in other books.

I have participated in numerous retreats and workshops that included the experience of praying with clay. What I learned from these retreats, and what I found "worked" for me are illustrated in these pages.

<u>REFLECTIONS IN CLAY: Mirror of Truth</u>, leads us into the deeper realms of our own body/spirit/soul where divine movement is sensed but not easily verbalized. Having touched in to a deeper place, shaped that space in clay, we then bring the experience to light by verbalizing our process.

<u>REFLECTIONS IN CLAY: Mirror of Truth</u> describes processes in a step-by-step format for the novice in tactile prayer, and for the prayer facilitator who wishes to lead a group of people into the wonders of praying with clay. The book provides much 'white space' for the reader/facilitator's notes and adaptation ideas. Every experience of praying with clay can be an adventure. In a step-by-step-how-to development, six easy to read chapters develop a background for praying with clay and lay out the beginning experience in great detail and then describe seven more possible uses of the basic procedures.

Chapter 4, Images, Prayers and Reflections, illustrates some of the author's own prayer in clay, and some reflections from her journal.

In Chapter 5 several participants share some of their reflections in praying with clay, and Chapter 6 contains reflections on centering our lives with the help of centering a pot on a wheel, and concludes with a folk tale from Native American spirituality as retold by Martha Bartholomew, author of the book, <u>Tellers of Story and Keeper of Dream.</u>

Abundant listings of resources used by the author, an annotated bibliography and a topical index expand the usefulness of this book.

TABLE OF CONTENTS

TABLE OF ILLUSTRATIONS

INTRODUCTION

My first experience of praying with clay was in 1983, while I was on retreat. At the age of 57, I was trying to explain to my Spiritual Director what was going on in my soul. The words would not come easily because I was so confused. This is what happened.

I had been getting deep into "FEMININE SPIRITUALITY." The deeper I went, the more disturbed and frightened I became. Much of what I was hearing and experiencing and reading directly contradicted the very fabric of my value structures. Such statements as

"I am WOMAN." "I have rights." "What I think is important." began to usurp the deeply implanted admonitions:

"You're only a girl." "You have no right!" "Who cares what you think!" which I had heard in one way or another much of my young years, and which I had internalized into a strong belief system.

I was confused. I was on retreat. And I was trying to tell my Spiritual Director/Retreat Companion what was happening to me. The words would not come out in any coherent expression, but I flailed along. Suddenly I realized she was asking me to stop talking, and

"Go into that room over there and get a ball of clay."

"Why?" I asked, mystified.

"I'd like you to just spend some time with it, playing with it, handling it."

"Why?" I continued to be mystified. Here I was pouring out my soul in total confusion, and she was asking me to get some CLAY!

"Just to see what happens," she persevered, knowingly.

THE TOUCH OF CLAY

I had spent a large portion of time during a sabbatical year not too long before, making pots on a wheel. This had been a centering time for me, and just touching the clay now evoked the healing sense I had experienced back then. I took the clay to my room and sat with it in my hands, feeling it, pressing it, rolling it and patting it. A calm pervaded my body as I relaxed into the ambience of the smooth, cool, yielding yet resisting texture of the clay.

TAKING SHAPE

Suddenly I became aware that the mass of earth between my hands was taking on the unmistakable shape of a woman. "Strange!" I thought, as I lost that image in a quickly re-shaped ball, and continued my exploration. Soon the woman-shape came again, and finally, the third time, I realized this is why my director, Sister Martha Buser, OSU had suggested I get the clay.

My body was more calm and my thoughts more peaceful. In fact, my confusion and fear began to abate, and I began to think clearly of qualities of WOMAN as each distinctive feature became more visible. As I continued to caress the clay, now with the clear intention to continue with the image of a woman's body, I lost a lot of the questions as no longer important. I found some answers, and I have come to live with many of the questions that don't seem to have any answers.

INNER IMAGE

I do not remember all the thoughts that accompanied this transformation of a lump of clay into a woman's body shape, but I do know that that experience was echoed in my interior. I began to realize the significance and real value of my own being as a woman, yes, today in today's church and society. Buried deep in the folds and layers of clay were the doubts and fears I had been experiencing. New life-giving thoughts replace the old messages:

IT IS GOOD THAT I AM A WOMAN.
I HAVE EVERY RIGHT TO EXIST.

The poem words "You are a child of the Universe, you have a right to be here" suddenly applied to me, and I truly believed that

WHAT I THINK *IS WORTHY OF BEING*
EXPRESSED AND SHARED.

Almost simultaneously with this strongly felt sense of my own worth, came a sense of *SOLIDARITY WITH OTHER WOMEN.* I am not alone in my uniqueness...Women have value for who they are. And I am one of them.

GOD IS MOTHER, ALSO

A third very exciting affirmation and validation came from this experience. In my studies and reflections on women's spirituality, liberation, development and historical and present-day oppression, I had also come to relate to some of the "feminine" qualities of God. The clay experience validated this spiritual movement in my life. The little figurine I now treasure from my first experience of praying with clay is a "formed in clay" (not "carved in stone!") image that conveys to me without apology or equivocation that God is Mother as well as Father.

PRAYING WITH CLAY

Needless to say, from that retreat onward, PRAYING WITH CLAY became an integral part of my spiritual life. When I returned from the retreat, I immediately searched out a source for clay. Whenever I had a block of time to devote to prayer I would become immersed in a new clay experience. Many of those first images were "woman" figures, each one helping me to firm up an aspect of my feminine qualities and approach to life.

I deepened my appreciation of the process of just sitting with a lump of clay and allowing my hands to dialogue with it until it has delivered its message for the day or time in my life. In times of trouble or confusion I would seek out my clay, experiencing again the calming influence it had had on my agitation. Each piece I formed in this way carries with it a "story" and significance for me. All I need to do is look at or touch one of them, to relive instantly the original experience of its creation. I am renewed, re-created in its spirit.

Also needless to say, the clay figurines began to accumulate, and overflow from bedroom to living room at home, and eventually to my office at work. Friends would notice them, ask about them, and some would say, "Oh, I want to do that too!"

FAITH SHARING

I began offering the experience first to personal friends, and gradually to others, using the parish bulletin to advertise PRAYING WITH CLAY AND IMAGINATION classes at St. Vincent de Paul Roman Catholic Church in Elkhart, Indiana, where I was Director of Religious Education from 1980 to 1989.

Soon individuals were not only experiencing new ways of praying, primarily imaging in prayer and praying with clay, but they were also beginning to share with me their spiritual journeys. When they would consult me about their prayer life or relationship with God, I would respond from my heart, and knew we were in a healthy spiritual relationship. I began to realize I was being called into a more intense form of spiritual consultation. To reassure myself this was indeed a calling, I consulted with other spiritual directors, close friends, and my religious superiors.

BY WHAT AUTHORITY?

The upshot of it all is that I entered the extension program in the SHALEM INSTITUTE OF SPIRITUAL FORMATION near Washington D.C. While continuing full time work at St. Vincent's I studied, reflected, and consulted under the able leadership of Gerald May. What had begun as a touchstone experience in my CLAY RETREAT became for me a whole new ministry. At the time of this writing, I am continuing the work I started then. It is my desire to pass on to others some of my experiences and ways of sharing this extraordinary way of praying. My religious superiors saw the value and validity of this calling and have been more than supportive in assisting me to answer the call.

Praying with clay is for me an important way of being with God, and with persons who come for spiritual consultation.

CHAPTER 1.

JUST WHAT IS PRAYING WITH CLAY
(And Why Would I?)

The life of prayer is perhaps the most mysterious dimension of all human experiences. For a long time, the prayer formulas we learned as children seem to have satisfied our need for prayer. Then gradually, we learned there is more to prayer than reciting words. We begin to sense that giving ourselves entirely to God cannot be restricted to a "time for prayer." God refuses to be compartmentalized, and we begin to know something is missing. We go to a prayer meeting, a liturgy, a session alone in the church and we feel empty, dry, cheated. "Nothing happened." I am no longer satisfied.

It seems this is nothing new in the history of our relationships with God. Many years ago, for example, Jeremiah may have been feeling disconnected, out of it, all dried up, when he got a special message from God:

> *"The word that was addressed to Jeremiah by Yahweh, 'Get up and make your way down to the potter's house; there I shall let you hear what I have to say.' So I went down to the potter's house; and there he was, working at the wheel. And whenever the vessel he was making came out wrong, as happens with the clay handled by potters, he would start afresh and work it into another vessel, as potters do. Then this word of Yahweh was addressed to me, 'House of Israel, cannot I do to you what this potter does? - it is Yahweh who speaks. Yes, as the clay is in the potter's hand, so are you in mine, House of Israel.'" (Jer.18: 1-6, Jerusalem Bible.)*

The fact that you are reading this book indicates to me that we have something in common, a desire to pray, even if it means submitting to God as a potter, one who works in clay. Who but God has had the greatest experience in molding the clay of the earth?

Another place in Scripture tells us that God scooped up the clay of the earth and formed it into God's own image and likeness, and then breathed into it God's own breath, thereby making this clay creation a living breathing human being. (Genesis 1 & 2) In this story God has just joined heaven and earth, spirit and flesh, breath and clay into this all new being, HUMANITY, of which we are members.

Now, here today many centuries later, we creatures of the Godhead seek to be in communion with our Creator. Hidden deep within each of our hearts lies an image, which brings us closer to God than we may ever have imagined. In praying with clay we let that creative energy that seems to be centered in our hands find an image in the clay which in turn may mirror this interior image of God for us.

The call to move inward is a gift to you and to me, of the One who calls, and who waits to be found within the inner passages and wondrous places you will discover in your own interior. Meditation with clay is a powerful way to move into our interior depths, to listen to our inner self and to become aware of the God who dwells within. Molding the clay without conscious thought or plan does not require "artistic talent" but only a willingness to be open to whatever comes. The product is not nearly as important as the process that can lead to a meditation and a message. Sometimes our hands can form in clay something we can't find words to express.

1

Marianne McGriffin, S.P.

With our hands we can shape our prayer for help, for healing, for relationship with our God. We who are ministers with persons who are in need of healing can shape our prayer for the help we need to become a healing presence to others.

Praying with clay can be a means of:

…Getting in touch with who we are,
…Touching our own substance,
…Imaging the God who dwells within each of us.

In praying with clay, I allow the creative energy that resides in my hands to find in the clay the image waiting there for me at this time in my life. As my hands "work" the clay, fondling and caressing it, I do not plan what I will make, but when I see a shape being formed I pay attention to it. I begin to "converse" with the image that is being formed. This process usually provides much for prayer and spiritual awareness. It has a calming effect on my body, mind and spirit.

Besides finding the inner image process described above, we can use clay in other ways of praying. One can reflect on a scripture passage or explore a dream by simply handling the clay while mulling over the passage or the dream. Often the process will awaken a new understanding of the passage, or the message in the dream may become clearer in this process. Clay can also be used to make intentional shapes such as pinch pots, Puja lamps, light holders, etc. for use in other prayer experiences.

Anyone can pray with clay, but it seems especially in harmony with the nature of woman. With clay, we may recognize a vital connection with Mother Earth. One might choose praying with clay to help integrate and concretize the varied experiences of life, especially in a time of turmoil, grief, or enrichment.

The process uses the sensate and intuitive functions of the soul, and can help one get in touch with elusive or buried feelings. By journaling the experience one can facilitate order in one's life through use of the thinking function and the decision-making powers of judgment. The person who is journaling may perceptively leave open the possibility of new development. Journaling can also be a means of deepening one's relationship with oneself, with others and with God, as it helps one to IMAGE the God in one's life.

PRAYING WITH CLAY CAN ALSO BE JUST PLAIN FUN!

TO PRAY WITH CLAY

*To pray with clay
Is to make friends with the earth,
To pick up the ball of clay, and touch it,
To feel it,
And squeeze it:
To know its response
And resistance to your touch.
To pray with clay
Is to become intimate with it,
To converse with it, and listen to it,
To breathe with it, and speak to it;
To let it speak to the innermost Being.
To pray with clay
Is to enter into the energy of the Universe;
To feel that creative energy in your hands;
To allow the energy to flow;
To let go, and to allow the IMAGE to form.
To pray with clay is to commune with God;
To come to know who you are;
To touch your own substance;
And to image the God within.
To pray with clay
Is to do what God does
With the clay that is ourselves.*

Marianne McGriffin, S.P.

CHAPTER 2

SEE WHAT HAPPENS

As described in more detail in the INTRODUCTION, the first time I prayed with clay was during a private retreat when my spiritual director gave me a ball of clay and said, "*See what happens.*" So much happened that day that I have been using clay as an aid to prayer ever since. That was in 1983.

In the ensuing years I have participated in numerous CLAY RETREATS or retreats that offered clay as an option for prayer. Sister Helen Buening's CLAY AND FIRE RETREAT offered many different opportunities along with reflections and how-tos for working and praying with clay. We even dug up our own clay from the side of a creek bed near Atchison, Kansas, and processed it by working the gritty, slimy earth through a sieve to remove bits of wood and rock. This experience taught me that "pure" clay might not always be usable for sculpting or making pots. Several kinds of clay need to be mixed together for strength and durability.

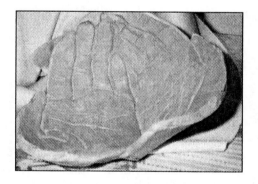

MY HANDS

MY CUP OVERFLOWS
Clay dug from the riverbed
By my hands
Overflowing with gifts
From God.
These hands cup the grace
To remember.

That day I replicated my own hands cupped to hold overflowing grace, but as the clay dried it disintegrated into dust. It could not hold its shape long enough to be fired. I still wanted to use my personally dug and processed clay, though, so I learned to add BALL CLAY to it for strength. I reshaped the hands, and still have them to remind me of the day my "cup overflows" as I experienced the wonders of creation in clay.

Marianne McGriffin, S.P.

This chapter is an attempt at sharing some of the things I learned from Sister Helen, and from others who offered clay as an aid to prayer during various retreats. Time has blurred the lines of demarcation between what someone else developed, and what I 'figured out for myself.' At any rate, here is how I introduce the praying with clay experience.

I. OVERVIEW OF FIRST SESSION

1. Materials needed check list
2. Before we begin
3. Introductory thoughts
4. Hand meditation
5. The clay
    Receiving it
    Getting acquainted with it
6. Everything that is...
7. Something I have learned
8. Proceeding on your own
9. Ending
    Reflection
    Hand washing ritual
    Sharing
10. Closing reflections with music
11. Nitty-Gritty

MATERIALS NEEDED:

❖ CLAY I use "RED CLAY", or "INDIAN RED CLAY" because I like the texture and the color. (Enough for each person to have one piece at least.) Other clay can be used, even self-hardening synthetic clays, modeling clay, Play-Doh, Sculpty or home made salt "clay". (See recipe in Appendix) I have the clay already cut into manageably sized pieces weighing about ¼ pound, or just big enough to hold in the palm of the hand. I keep the clay pliable by wrapping it in wet towels and storing it in plastic bags and airtight containers. I have purchased the ready to use clay from a ceramics store or a school arts supply store.

❖ CARDBOARDS (I started out with cut up corrugated squares about 5 inches by 5 inches. Later a friend provided me with cut up matting board. It just has to be stiff enough to hold the finished piece. Later, I started using small paper plates.

❖ PAPER TOWELS (To protect the table, lap or floor. Crumbs do dry on the hands and fall.)

❖ PAN OF HOT SOAPY WATER, TOWELS, and LOTION for after the clay has been formed, to wash and dry hands, and protect them from drying out.

❖ SANDWICH BAGS to cover the finished piece, to allow it to dry slowly.

❖ TAPE PLAYER, EXTENSION CORD, AND ALL TAPES TO BE USED FOR MUSIC. I will name the tapes I use, but you may wish to choose your own music. (If you are able to provide "live" music, that is even better.)

❖ LOW TABLE, PREFERABLY ROUND, DECORATIVE CLOTH, CANDLE. (I arrange the paper towels and cardboards around the candle on the table, and have chairs arranged around the table in a circle. I find most manageable five to fifteen participants.)

II. BEFORE WE BEGIN

After all participants are assembled seated in a circle, INTRODUCTIONS are made. (Name, why came, expectations, etc.) Preliminary remarks include where the bathroom is, what the above named things are there for, and any icebreaker comments such as, "When is the last time you had your hands in clay?" Also, I ask them to make a prayerful ritual of the washing of hands to thank hands for what they have done today, and using the lotion for a grateful massage.

III. INTRODUCTORY THOUGHTS

I tell briefly the story of how I got started praying with clay: (A brief summary of the INTRODUCTION.) Of course this will not be your story. You may wish to share something from YOUR first experience of praying with clay.

(Other suggested openers are given in the APPENDIX.)

HANDS

*Remember, God has no other hands than ours
To touch others, to create, to build.
The OPEN HAND signifies PEACE, LOVE, GIVING.
The CLOSED HAND denotes WAR, hate, greed.*

HANDS

*Are spoken of eight hundred fifty times
Or more in the Bible.*

PRAISE GOD FOR HANDS.

(Helen of Atchison)

IV. HAND MEDITATION

I ask participants to look at their hands, held out, palms up, fingers splayed.

"Place all your awareness in your hands."

"As you gaze at your hands, let your imagination remember these same hands as they were many years ago, when they were so tiny they could barely wrap themselves around an adult's thumb, and how they would cling with all of their infant might...

"Recall some of the ways your hands have served you from the first moment of your life until now...

"...How it was your tiny hands that at some time grasped at a chair leg, held on tightly, and pulled your whole body up onto your wobbly legs and helped you to take that first step...

"...How it was your hands that helped you learn your numbers and letters, did your homework and your chores, learned the power of loving touch and of angry striking out...

"...Recall just today the many things your hands have done from the moment you woke up until you got here today...

"How precious to us are these hands we have before us!

"...Be present to your hands.

"...You may begin to notice the air passing between your fingers...you may feel in the palms of your hands a sensation you'd never noticed before...

"...Some would say it's the pressure of the air you are feeling in a way you don't normally feel it. Or perhaps it's the creative energy that always resides there, and now is stirring, to be released in the creative act of praying with clay...

"...And just to remind us that we are not the first to ever pray with clay, I call forth the story in Genesis which tells us that God scooped up the clay and fashioned the first human form, and breathed into that form the very breath of God, and the clay figure became alive.

"...In remembrance of that moment of creation, I ask you to breathe upon your own hands, as a way of stirring up the creative power that resides there in your palms."

V. THE CLAY: RECEIVING IT

I will come and place a piece of clay in your palms. Just hold them as they are now, fully attending to them. As you receive the clay, just hold it there, and notice how it feels—its weight, its temperature...Be aware of how YOU feel just holding that lump of clay before you...Please continue to hold it until all have received theirs.

GETTING ACQUAINTED WITH IT

Let's begin to move it from one hand to the other, noticing how it feels...Press it, notice what happens...Squeeze it, notice what happens...Pull it...Push it...Do whatever comes naturally to mind to do with it...Notice all the time how it feels, and how you feel about how it feels.

Someone has said that EVERYTHING THAT IS can speak to us of God. And I would add, can speak to us of our relationship with God, and with one another. SOMETHING I HAVE LEARNED, just by holding a piece of clay, is that if I were to leave this piece of clay on a windowsill someplace and go away and forget about it for a couple of weeks, when I came back, it would be dry and hard, and probably cracked.

This tells me something about human relationships. If I neglect them, they are likely to dry up and even break...

But clay also tells me is that even broken relationships can sometimes be mended—just by the kindness, thoughtfulness, forgiveness and caring that we have all learned go into mending a broken relationship. Broken, dry clay can be put back together by softening it with water, handling it gently, coating the broken edges with softened wet clay and pressuring the broken pieces together. So, too, a broken relationship can be mended.

Something else I have learned is that by now your handprints are all over the clay, and the clay is also all over your hands—just as God's handprints are all over us, and our handprints are all over one another. We do make impressions on every person who comes into contact with us.

You may come up with your own learning just from handling the clay in the way we are doing now. I ask you to continue doing just what you are doing now, paying close attention to what is going on in the clay and in you.

As you continue handling the clay, you may notice that it begins to 'look like something.' When this happens, you may wish to stay with it and continue more consciously to make it what it looks like. Or you may wish to continue exploring. Sometimes your shape is not recognizable, but it feels right. Pay attention to your own process.

You will have a sense when to stop. But just to allay your concerns about time and getting finished, I will say that it takes sometimes twenty minutes or more. You may have finished before that, or may not be finished. Don't worry. If we run out of time, I will call you back even with your unfinished piece. Even that is something to pay attention to.

VI. CONFUSIONS, A QUESTION, COMMENTS

The most frequently asked question at this point is WHAT IF NOTHING HAPPENS?

I simply say if nothing seems to be happening, just let go of trying to MAKE it happen, and PLAY WITH THE CLAY. It's OK if nothing happens. Just be aware of how it feels if nothing is happening, and be ready to say that when it is time to share. Then, JUST PLAY WITH IT.

VII. PROCEEDING ON YOUR OWN

I will stop talking, and you are on your own. When I start the music you may feel free to move to another part of the room if you wish. Just please continue doing what you are doing. Feel the rhythm of the music...'Dance' with it...'Listen' to what is happening in the clay and in you. Remember, "EVERYTHING THAT IS CAN SPEAK TO US OF GOD."

(I use RAINBOW PATH music. See Resources.)

VIII. ENDING AND SHARING

After about 20 minutes I look around to assess the progress. Some are finishing, and going to wash their hands. Others begin to follow. When all or most have returned to their places and are reflecting or journaling in silence, I call any stragglers to come, finished or not, and begin to share.

I usually start the sharing by picking up my piece from the table, holding it in my hand, and sharing my process and reflections briefly.

Then I ask others to share 'as the spirit moves,' by picking up their piece and saying whatever they feel comfortable sharing about their process and/or the significance of the piece to them.

(I AM CONSTANTLY IMPRESSED AND TOUCHED BY THE VARIETY OF PIECES SHOWN AND SHARED. THE SHARING RANGES FROM BRIEF AND SIMPLE TO DEEP AND DETAILED AS TO THE SIGNIFICANCE OF EACH PIECE.)

As each one shares, I say a simple 'thank you' and wait for the next one to share. When all who wish to have shared, I ask if anyone has seen or heard anything that especially touches THEM, e.g. "Your lovely rose reminds me of how much I love roses and what they mean to me..." This sharing is done briefly and without interpreting the piece for the creators, only what it means to 'me'. I do not encourage discussion, but only simple sharing.

IX. CLOSING REFLECTION WITH MUSIC

I say, "To close off the prayer aspect of this experience I would like you to continue holding your piece in your hand as we listen to the song, 'Earthen Vessels' and look around at one another." I like to ritualize a blessing by asking them to look at each person's face, then at their piece, then back at the face, as a way of affirming, blessing and thanking that person for participating and sharing.

X. NITTY-GRITTY

What to do with your piece:
1. If you want to keep it:
   ❖ Put it where you can see it, and allow it to continue speaking to you.
   ❖ Let it dry for about two weeks by covering it with a small 'tent' of plastic. (I use sandwich bags split down one side. DEMONSTRATE.)
   ❖ Keep your piece on the cardboard to allow the bottom to dry slowly also.
   ❖ It can be fired slowly to cones 06-05
   ❖ After firing, it can be - left as it is
        - coated with a clear wax
        - glazed
        - or painted with acrylic paint.
2. If you want to re-shape your clay
   ❖ Do not fire it
   ❖ Wrap it in an absorbent wet cloth and a tightly closed plastic bag. This will allow the clay to take moisture from the cloth and become pliable again.
   ❖ After a day or two check and see if it is soft enough or needs more moisture.
3. If you want to recycle your piece now before you leave, just drop it in the barrel.
4. If you'd like another piece of clay to take with you, please do. (I have more available, and plastic bags to wrap it in.)
5. If your piece is very thick and you want to fire it, you will need to make some air holes. I use a piece of wire coat hanger, and while the clay is still soft, insert the wire up through the bottom and through the thickest part in one or two places. This will allow to escape any steam that builds up during the firing. Otherwise, the piece may explode in the kiln.

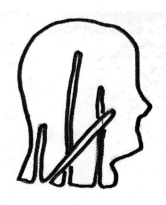

FOR THICK PIECES

Marianne McGriffin, S.P.

CHAPTER 3

OTHER PRAY WITH CLAY EXPERIENCES

1. PUJA LAMPS

A PUJA POT

Needs a small ball of clay
The size of an English walnut.

This is placed in the palm of the hand,
Gently rotated around until a small round bowl is
Shaped.
With the thumb and forefinger, press one area of
The rim together
To form a V or a U shape which catches and holds the
Wick.
After firing, use a heavy cotton string in
Vegetable oil as wick,
And when lighted,
A PRAYER LAMP.
(Helen of Atchison)

    This little lamp is inspired by a small oil lamp someone gave me which is said to be over 1000 years old. Some have said that the Hindus use a similar lamp in a prayer in which a dancer holds a lighted one in each hand and moves in rhythm to music. Others have said that the lamp was used in the Middle East in prayer somewhat as we use candles today.

13

I. MATERIALS NEEDED

- ❖ Small lemon-size balls of clay.
- ❖ Tea lamps sufficient for the group.
- ❖ Small squares of cardboard
- ❖ Large candle in center of table
- ❖ Book of matches with enough matches for each to have one match.
- ❖ Table covered with decorative cloth.
- ❖ Small receiver for spent matches.
- ❖ Copies of the *"Prayer of Light and Splendor,"* from <u>PRAYERS FOR THE DOMESTIC CHURCH,</u> by Ed Hayes.

II. PREPARATION

Arrange table with large candle lighted in center and individual tea lamps arranged in a circle around the candle. The cardboards can be arranged in the circle also. The receiver can be next to the large candle.

(I have found this short activity ideal for closing off a day of retreat, or as a movement into retreat the evening before the first full day of a retreat. Or it can be a separate prayer activity. It is especially effective when the room can be darkened.)

III. THE EXPERIENCE

Here's how I lead the PUJA LAMP activity:

I say," The Hindus have a lamp they use somewhat as we use candles for our prayer. We can make a prayer lamp (Puja lamp) for ourselves right now."

All are in a circle. "Because our hands are taking on the work of the creator, we call upon the Spirit to be present in our hands. I will breathe upon your hands (Or each person breathes on their own hands) as a reminder of the breath of God breathing life into Adam and Eve."

(Present each one with a small ball of clay about the size of a small lemon. Demonstrate each of the following steps.)

- ❖ Start by making a simple pinch pot.
- ❖ First, shape the clay into a true ball—just as round as you can make it. You may need to pat it some to round it out.
- ❖ Second, when your ball is as round as you can make it, use your thumb to impress the center of the ball on one side.
- ❖ Then, holding the ball between that thumb and the first two fingers of the same hand, continue to impress with the thumb, and pinch with the fingers while at the same time rotating the ball of clay with the other hand, so that the thumb stays in the same spot, but the finger move around the clay, pinching evenly all the way around.
- ❖ Try not to stretch it out too far. You can start over again if you want. The clay responds as you treat it. If it begins to crack on the edge, use saliva (<u>not water</u>) to moisten and smooth the edge. Water can make it crack worse.

❖ Continue turning and pinching until it begins to look like a small bowl. Keep pressing and turning, pulling out and up on sides till you have a satisfying round dish—one whose sides are reasonably even in thickness, and not very deep. Check to see if one of the tea lamps will fit inside it, and adjust accordingly.

❖ Put your mark on it—date and initials, some insignia, a ring setting, a tree, flower or music note.

❖ When you are satisfied, hold the bowl in one hand, and with thumb and first finger of the other, pinch a small spout on one side of the bowl.

❖ Now we have our lamp.

❖ Place in it one of the tea lamps from the table, and put the finished product on a small cardboard in a circle around the main candle. (*I use tea lamps instead of oil and wick, simply because it is easier to have a clean burning wick. Oil may burn too fast, and cause smoke.*)

❖ Place the finished product on a small cardboard in a circle around the main candle. *When all are satisfied, allow each, one at a time, to light their lamp from the Christ Candle in the center.*

❖ As you light your candle, please use the match you have taken from the book of matches, light it from the Christ Candle, and speak some word about light in your life, asking for light, saying how you need light, asking Jesus to be your light, etc.

❖ Place the burnt match in the container provided.

IV. GUIDED MEDITATION

"Let's move a little deeper into our own centers. Continue to look at your own lamp flame, or at the Christ Candle in the center of the table. Be aware only of the flame...

"Close your eyes, and sink down into the very center of your being. See the tiny flame that is there. If you can't actually see it, imagine that you do, and allow it to grow until it fills your whole being...

"Imagine the light growing until it not only fills your whole being, but also escapes from you into the room. All of our lights now meld into one great light, which spreads beyond this room into the whole house...it fills the house and moves out into the city...town...country...into the whole universe...

"Let us let the light of Christ radiate out from us into the entire world and universe, bringing light into the darkness."

V. SILENT REFLECTION

(Close the prayer by reciting the "Prayer of Light and Splendor" (*See Appendix*) or some other prayer of your choice and/or sing a "Light" hymn such as "The Light Shines On."*(See Appendix)*

VI. NITTY GRITTY

The lamps can be kept and used as is, but they must be allowed to dry slowly by covering them with the plastic "tent" lest they crack and break.

I am sure you can think of other ways of using the Puja Lamp to fit whatever occasion you choose.

One last thing I often say is, "Do you remember how your match flared up when it was held to the Christ Candle? And then how it softened to steady flame? It may be that your own fervor has been brightened by this prayer time together. May your flame of love, flared up during this time, continue to burn steadily in your life. And if it seems to go out, please do enter into another retreat or prayer experience to allow your fervor to be re-lit."

2. IMPRESSIONS

I. INTRODUCTION

> *We are transformed, not by adopting attitudes toward ourselves but by bringing into center all the elements of our sensations; our thinking and our emotions and our will, all the realities of our bodies and our souls; all the dark void in us of our undiscovered selves, all the small light of our discovered being, all the drive of our hungers. Our fairest and darkest dreams, all, all the elements come into center, into union with all other elements.*
> *And in such a state they become quite different in function than when they are separated and segregated and discriminated between or against. When we act out of an inner unity, when all of ourselves is present in what we do, then we can be said to be 'ON CENTER.'*
> ***THE CLAY IS A VERY SELFISH MEDIUM. IT ASKS FOR TOTAL SELF-GIVING.***
> *(Helen of Atchison)*

In this session, we make a small plaque honoring someone who has influenced our lives in a remarkable way. This plaque may also remind us of a book or an event in our lives we wish to commemorate.

II. MATERIALS NEEDED:

❖ Sturdy table (s) (Picnic tables out doors are ideal)
❖ Larger portions of clay (about one pound)
❖ Newspaper (lots of it)
❖ Cardboards about 8 ½ by 12 inches.
❖ Lighted Candle
❖ Some samples of plaques already made.
❖ Collection of small objects that might be used for making impressions: nuts, shells, twigs, buttons, necklaces with interesting shaped links and/or beads, chains—anything with texture. I also have a potato ricer to use to make "hair", "grass," or "bird nests."
❖ Some incising tools such as styli or pencils,
❖ A special tool for making holes for hanging the plaque when finished.
❖ 'Alphabet Soup' letters
❖ Pan and soapy water, towels, and lotion for washing and massaging hands when finished.

III. PREPARATION

I start out saying something like this: "Everything that is in our lives makes an impression on us. In this session we remember persons who have made a deep impression on our lives."

Sometimes I ask participants to bring with them some small object, or to go outside and walk in nature observing everything around them and to bring back some small nature object, (a rock, leaf, twig, shell, blossom) which reminds them of someone important in their lives.

I play the song "*Listen*" (See Appendix) after suggesting some time of silence, listening to our own hearts. Reflection question: What object do you have that reminds you of someone or some event?

In a few minutes, I ask them to look around at the objects on the table that might also be used to remind them of that person or event or book. I say,

"Just walk around the table, remembering the person, and pick up something and hold it for a moment. You may put it down and pick up something else, or keep it to use for an impression. There are also 'alphabet soup' letters you may choose to make a word or phrase."

When we are ready, I demonstrate how to "slab" the clay to make a natural, flat shape on which to impress their objects. I throw the clay down hard on several layers of newspaper. We use the newspaper so that the clay will not stick to the table. It can be peeled off, and the clay turned over and thrown down again and again until it has a thickness no less than ¼ inch, and the shape we want.

Because the clay is composed of tiny platelets, it spreads out in layers whenever we drop it or throw it down. Hold on to the paper! Each time you peel the clay from the paper, turn it over and throw it down again until you have a shape that satisfies you.

This may be a good time to remember a bad or difficult experience, a time when you wanted to strike out and hit somebody or something, but didn't because it wasn't proper or ladylike...That feeling got buried in your own clay, and it may be good to RELEASE it by throwing this clay down hard.

Keep throwing the clay until it has a nice shape. You can always roll it up and start over. When you are satisfied, take the objects you picked up and make impressions—pleasing designs. This again can be done over as often as you wish. You may repeat the impression or add other impressions as you are moved to do so. Make a hole or two with the hole-maker so that later on you can run a cord through the hole(s) and hang the plaque on the wall.

When your plaque is finished you can tear the paper around it and transfer paper and clay to a cardboard so it is easier to carry without destroying your shape.

All gather in a circle and place their plaques around the candle in the middle of the table.

IV. SHARING

Each one may share their plaque, what it means to them, who it represents, what the design may mean to them in a prayerful way, more as prayer than as a discussion.

V. CLOSING:

A SONG, SUCH AS *"Like a Seal on Your Heart"* or another of your choice may be used to bring this session to a reflective close.

VI. NITTY GRITTY

After the plaque has dried a little, you may wish to turn it over and inscribe your name and the date on the back.

- ❖ Again, cover it with a "tent" of plastic, and keep it on the cardboard allowing it to dry slowly.
- ❖ The piece can be fired slowly to cone 05-06, or just left as is. A cord can be strung through the hole or holes, to create a hanger for it.
- ❖ This plaque makes a lovely gift for the person being honored.

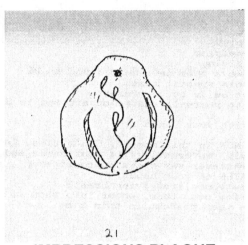

IMPRESSIONS PLAQUE
We ought to imprint all God's gifts in our hearts
(Mechtild of Magdeburg)

3. KAIROS

In this experience, we focus our energies on integrating experiences of the day, series, retreat, etc. by seeking to find an image for NOW. The process is similar to INNER IMAGE experience, but with the present moment in focus.

I. and II. PREPARATION and MATERIALS NEEDED

Similar to **INTRODUCTORY SESSION**

III. INTRODUCTION

NOW in this moment, we will make present a sacred time, KAIROS, God's time, Your time, ONE TIME.

IV. HAND MEDITATION

Hold your hands in the receiving way, and be present to them. Know how they experience you now—in this moment.

Let your hands remember the things they have done in the past two months (days or hours)—the work, the play, the helping, the giving, the ways they have helped you to BE in this special time, set aside to be present to yourself and to others and to God.

Be with your hands...

And NOW in this moment, God's time, KAIROS, Slowly, reverently lift your hands and in whatever way seems appropriate, BREATHE on your hands, allowing your life-giving breath to blow over them, enter into them, make them present in this time...

V. RECEIVING THE CLAY

(With a large group, this way of getting the clay may be used;) Ask each and all together, to slowly, reverently, presently follow one another around in a complete circle. Starting here, pick up your clay and move on around the circle, moving with time, being present to your clay.

When you come back to your starting point sit down and begin exploring your clay.

Hold it...Feel it...Reverence it.

In rhythm with the music move with your clay.

(Play the tape, *"Listen,"* (See appendix.) as they begin being with their clay, and then put on *"Rainbow Path."*

VI. SHARING

as in other experiences

VII. CLOSING SONG

after all have shared: *"You Are Near"*, or other song.

> *Take the ball of clay and explore, search, and live inside it*
> *In order to meet the form that inhabits it.*
> *With your fingers and your hands search for the shape*
> *Hidden inside the clay.*
> *Close your eyes and allow your sense of touch to guide you.*
> *As you work with the clay, it works with you,*
> *Often giving insight and a sudden change in*
> *Direction that you are not expecting.*
> *(Maria Harris)*

4. LOVING CUP

Observe the way you hold a cup or a mug.
How does it feel in your hand, or hands?
How does your body feel?
This love mug calls upon other qualities
Beyond a simple pot and will produce new insights.
We concentrate on our feelings, our connectedness.
We follow our inner and outer relatedness, our wholeness.
Think of this mug being used at a time when you are alone:
A personal time, an intimate time.
What kind of handle does it need?
Does it need a handle?
(Helen of Atchison)

I. GUIDED OBJECT MEDITATION

I say something like this: "Please sit as erect as you can, with your feet flat on the floor. Your hands can be in your lap, extended palms up. Begin to be aware of your breathing. Feel your whole body breathing.

"Check any tension points in your body. Press your eyes closed tightly for a few seconds then release them, freeing your forehead of any tension. Let your head tip forward in slow motion to relax the tension muscles in your neck. Begin to experience your whole body smiling. Feel how good it is to be here, breathing the breath of God.

"I will come and place a ball of clay into your open hands. Please just sit and hold the clay there, feeling its weight and temperature. Notice how you feel just holding this little lump of clay.

"Begin to explore it gently with your fingers. Notice how your closed eyes cannot see its firmness or softness, its flexibility or resistance, its roughness or smoothness. Be aware of how the clay takes on your warmth, how it contracts or expands.

"Raise the clay to your cheek, and notice how it feels as you touch your cheek with it. Hold it near your ear and listen for its sound. Now draw it near your nose and detect its unique scent. Now lower your hands, holding the clay, to your lap and reflect: Everything is a gift of God's love, goodness, wonder and beauty. There is nothing in all of creation that has not been an occasion for our recognizing the power and presence of God.

"Our prayer today is with Love.

"I have heard it said, "The three most dangerous words we can say are 'I love you.' I wonder why.

"I guess I can say it without meaning it, and make a mockery of love, or I can really mean it, and the consequences may be beyond all expectations.

"Love is like fire—uncontrolled, it is hazardous. It is passion. It is a power that binds us together.

"We will make a simple pot, by pinching, (as we did with the Puja Lamp,) but this time it will be larger, and be more like a cup. We'll call it our LOVING CUP."

II. SHAPING THE LOVING CUP

First, we make a smooth round ball of the clay we have in our hands. Roll it between your hands, 'pit it and pat it' until it has an even roundness. (Demonstrate.)

"HOW IS THIS BALL A SYMBOL OF MY LOVE?"

We will Impress one side of the ball with a thumb, then holding the ball between that thumb and two fingers, we move around the circle impressing the same spot with the thumb, and pinching up around the thumb with the two fingers. The other hand serves as a table on which to continue turning the clay. (Demonstrate)

Is it a cup yet? Does it need a handle? Two handles? No handle? To make a handle, simply pinch the pot on one side enough to squeeze out a holding piece. You may leave it solid or bring your finger through it to make a 'traditional' handle. (Demonstrate.)

It depends on how you will hold your cup. Will you caress it between two hands? Hold it with one hand, or pass it to your loved one to hold with the other handle? (Demonstrate)

WHAT IS THE SHAPE OF YOUR LOVE? OF YOUR LOVING CUP? WHAT SYMBOLS WILL YOU PUT ON THE OUTSIDE OF IT?

A message of love?

❖ Your name and your friend's name?
❖ Symbols for those you love?
❖ A passage from Scripture?

III. FURTHER REFLECTION

Gather round the prayer table, holding your cup in your two hands. Breathe deeply, quietly. Let your cup speak to you; touch you. Be present to it and all the love it represents.

Listen to a reading from 1 Corinthians, 13: 4-7,13.

Listen to another reading on love. My favorite is in **SEASONS OF YOUR HEART**, by Macrina Wiederkehr, on pp. 74-75. (*See Appendix*)

IV. SHARING may be done now, with each one simply saying what is in his/her heart.

V. CLOSING SONG may be "*Like a Seal on Your Heart.*"(*See Appendix*)

5. COMMUNITY

Clay forms are the breath of your own spirit, your love. Many similar clay forms (modules) bound together, pressed together may have a religious significance. (We the many are one in Christ.) A family, a church with one stone, one module symbolizing Christ the cornerstone.

I. MATERIALS NEEDED

1. Pictures, slides or the real object: wheat   trees   flowers   families   wheel   Rodin's Cathedral (in an art book?) Earth as seen from space.
2. Clay in larger portions than usual, about a pound in weight.
3. "Hump molds:" objects over which to drape your slabbed clay—dishes, bowls, plates, cups, stones.
4. "Stamps:" Seeds, buttons, other nature objects or pre-shaped clay stamps.
5. Tape—"We are Many Parts," "One Bread, One Body," or other appropriate songs
6. Tape player

II. RODIN'S CATHEDRAL

This sculpture piece of two hands called The Cathedral.
Why? Because he has two right hands
Thrust upward and touching;
A man and a woman who through their love
bring forth a family, a home, a church, and a cathedral.
A single piece of clay is easier to control but limited in scope.
To join two pieces of clay together, two persons together,
Two lovers as one in an intimate encounter,
Creates a new challenge.
Each demands the right firmness to sustain the weight of the other,
To build, to hold together, to be empty of self, a useful vessel.
Take two like formed pieces of clay,
Join them together to make a void, a total darkness.
Pierce, penetrate, open.
Light enters and reveals a useful
Open, empty space.
(Helen of Atchison)

III. REFLECTIONS

On examples of Community:
Picture or slide of many ROCKS on a riverbank.

Indians did not claim to own LAND. It was there for them to use and then to move on.

WHEAT has many segments, one stalk. Many grains of wheat are ground together to make flour for food.

TREES, FLOWERS have many parts but are single plants. Many different kinds of tree.

"E PLURIBUS UNUM"

SCRIPTURE: "The multitude that believe were united, heart and soul."(Acts 4: 32)

- ❖ ASTRONAUTS saw no boundaries when they looked down on the WORLD from space. Though many, we are one.
- ❖ Rodin's CATHEDRAL: Two right hands thrust upward and touching, a man and a woman who through their lives bring forth a family, a home, a church, a cathedral.
- ❖ A WHEEL is one circle, one hub, many spokes.

❖ We though many are one in Christ.

We create a unity made from many parts. Clay forms are the breath of our own spirit, our love. Many clay forms pressed together become an entity. One from many.

Two equal pieces

One from two

Community modules

IV. PROCEDURE

❖ Bless Hands
❖ Find a "hump mold" over which to drape and shape a slab of clay.
❖ Flatten out or "slab" by throwing down hard on a paper on the table a double portion of clay. Drape it over a "hump mold."
❖ Keep rim wet with damp cloth or paper towel while you make small balls of clay.
❖ Use buttons, "stamps" nut shells, or other nature objects to flatten out the small balls of clay.
❖ Overlap these around the lip of the base you made on the hump mold.
❖ Allow each of these stamped circles to represent someone in your life. All together they make one—family, community, or circle of friends.

V. SHARING

After shapes have been made, allow each person to share what has been made, and significance of stamped pieces and how they fit together.

VI. CLOSING: "One Bread, One Body,"

6. A NEW CREATION

You can do many things with clay...
Push this way and pull that way,
Squeeze and roll and attach and hollow.
But you can't do EVERYTHING with it.
You can go only so far and then the clay resists.
We come to know ourselves by our resistances.
The life you find in the clay will bring
A new birth of your ideals.
Some secret center within you becomes vitalized
As you work in clay
And in the art of transforming clay, earth clay...human clay.
(Helen of Atchison)

I. OPENING REFLECTION

We all breathe the spirit of our lives into what we make. It's not a talent we either have or don't have. We all breathe. We are all alive. We all have unique qualities. Yet it takes hard conscious and unconscious work to find our pot, and the freedom that each must seek is not one that lets me do what I want to do but rather a freedom that equips me to be able to do what I need to do.

II. PROCEDURES

This follows pretty closely the Procedures in the Opening Session.
I have used a slide meditation with the song, "*You Are Near.*" See Resources.
Give each one a ball of clay to handle as you talk of the qualities of clay.
We will let the clay take its natural shape. In nature, clay is formed in layers. You may slab it or roll it out or make a pinch pot. End up with a vessel of some kind pleasing to you.

III. SHARING

When all are finished take time to share how it all came about. HOW ARE WE like the clay, like earthen vessels?

IV. CLOSING SONG

Play the tape, "*Earthen Vessels.*" (See Resources)
God is abundance; His gifts beyond measure.
My heart is bewildered.
Afraid to hold such a treasure.
(A. Silesius p. 104)

7. BLIND SPOTS AND PUJA LAMPS

(A reflection on John 9:2-41)
This is one example of using clay while reflecting on a scripture passage.
I distribute the clay BEFORE reading the scripture, and ask the participants to handle the clay while I read the story and the reflection questions. I ask them to pay attention to what it is that JESUS does, and what the PEOPLE do. Because the passage is so long, I have selected verses which seem to carry the story without too much detail.

I. READING

JOHN 9: 2-9, 18-21, 24-25, 33-41.

II. REFLECTION

It seems to me that the people are more taken up with the moral status of the man born blind who now sees, than in the miracle which Jesus has just worked.
They are **BLIND** to what Jesus does, and they are **NOT** astounded with the healing effected by the clay Jesus made into mud with his spittle...
Their questions show **THEIR** blindness, and capture **OUR** attention...

"Isn't this the man we have seen begging?" (And I might add, whom we **KNOW** is a **SINNER** because of his **ILL FORTUNE**.)...

'**I AM THE MAN,**' He says, (who was blind and begging.)

But they are still not astounded by the miracle, only intent on denying what they see before their very eyes...

How often do we find ourselves, when confronted with someone who has experienced some misfortune—(**AIDS**, for example) asking the **ACCUSING QUESTION**—'Who has sinned, this person or another?' instead of opening our eyes to see with compassion the plight of the person before us!

'No sin,' Jesus replies, 'but that God's work might show forth'...(in US, I'd like to suggest,) because he goes on to say, 'We must do the deeds of the God who sent me, (the **DEEDS OF LIGHT IN THE DARK WORLD OF SIN AND SUFFERING**...)

And when he had used his own healing spittle to make mud of the clay at his feet, and made the blind man to see, the people who saw refused to see the work of God...

They refused to believe their own eyes, and would not accept the testimony of his parents, who though they admitted this man was their son, would not take a stand and proclaim the work of Jesus...

They all treated the healed man with suspicion and contempt: 'What? You are steeped in sin from your birth, and you are giving **US** lectures!'

Jesus exonerates the man, evokes from him a true act of faith, and reminds all of *us* who may self righteously *deny* our sight and the works of the God who works in our lives, that 'If we were truly blind, there would be no sin in that, but because we say we see, and close our eyes, our own sin is evident.'

+++++++++++++++++++++++++++++++

How like these people we are at times!

- ❖ They couldn't *believe* the change in this man. They suffered from a blindness of their own.
- ❖ We too suffer from blind spots. Our vision often is blurred when it comes to seeing *ourselves* as we really are.
- ❖ We suffer from many blind spots. Or we see others with a jaded eye. Or our parish/congregation, drawn together by God to carry on the MISSION of Jesus to *reveal* the love of God, we see as lacking in love, or narrow minded and self-centered.
- ❖ Let's reflect on the blindness we may suspect in ourselves, and be assured there is healing for us. Often the beginning of healing *is in desiring it.*
- ❖ Have we not said to ourselves questions like those the people asked?
- ❖ 'Isn't this the same klutzy me? Can I really do this new ministry?' (In our hearts we may say '***Yes, I am, and I can, because I have come to accept myself as who I am!***')
- ❖ Or '***Isn't this the same crabby person I knew so many years ago?***' (if the person were to hear our question, their answer might be, "***Yes, I am, but I have mellowed through the years.***"
- ❖ Or, 'Isn't this the same (community/parish/class) I have had problems with before? ('***Yes, we are, but we know that growth happens when we honestly face the tensions we experience,***' the group might answer.)

III. SILENT PAUSE

(still presumably handling the clay, bringing it to some satisfying form.)

IV. SHARING

Now look at the piece of clay you have been handling during this time of reading and reflection. Take a few minutes more to reflect on the piece as it is, change it if you wish, then we will share any reflections we may have.

(After all have shared what their piece represents to them...)

'Because God comes to us in the blessing and the trials, the hurts and the healings we share with one another, we may want to acknowledge our blind spots to one another, and express the desire to have them removed.'

One way we can signify this desire for true sight, and for healing is to take with us a little piece of clay, and let it be a reminder to us of the healing power that Jesus will exert on us if we ask with faith.

Each one could receive or take a small piece of clay, using the words

"LORD, THAT I MAY SEE HOW YOU ARE PRESENT IN MY LIFE, NO MATTER WHAT THE CIRCUMSTANCES."

V. CLOSING:

The experience could end with this ritual, or the clay they receive may be big enough for them to make a Puja Lamp, and the prayer could end with a prayer for light as described in the PUJA LAMP experience earlier in the book.

A closing song might be "*Great Things Happen.*"

CHAPTER 4

IMAGES, PRAYERS, AND REFLECTIONS

Herein follows a description of some of my own experience of praying with clay.

THE WAITING GOD
Inner woman-spirit emerges in clay as we co-create a new way of life.

Forming clay images and imaging in prayer seem to have gone hand in hand in my spiritual development. Take, for example, that first image of a woman that I made in the 1985 retreat in Louisville. In going back over my journal entries for the months preceding that retreat, I discovered that the woman I had formed in clay *was* the woman whom I discovered while exploring my inner caves two years previously:

I see a shadow…a movement…a shape.
A woman sits beside a fire.
I approach slowly, somewhat fearfully.
She is expecting me. She looks up. The fire is reflected in her eyes.
'I am she, and I've been waiting for you to come.'
'Here I am…I am lost…I don't know where to turn.'
'Stay here for a while. Sit here by the fire with me.'
(From journal notes, May 27, 1983, hereafter indicated by "J" and the date.)

Other feminine images followed one after another. "I AM" was a conscious effort to shape the form of Klaske Franck as she stood regally on stage at Notre Dame in Frederick Franck's play of <u>EVERYONE</u>, stating "*I am*," and portraying God, while Frederick himself had the role of 'Everyone.' I was so deeply touched, I remember saying '*I'm so glad God is a woman in this play!*'

"*I AM!*" she says, "for everyone a Mother." (J,7,85)

TIJUANA WOMAN

The only day in my life that I spent as a tourist in Tijuana, Mexico, evoked this figure of a Mexican woman who carried her infant on her back as she and her young daughter hawked souvenirs on the streets. I was attracted to her, and wanted to take her picture. She turned her back, refusing me a 'good shot.' I was offended, but could not get her out of my mind. Finally, back home in Indiana, my uneasiness with the situation found expression in my forming the three of them in clay. The process of replicating what I saw and experienced provided me the inner presence I needed to come to realize it was she whose space had been invaded. My thought was 'She did not want to be taken home as a souvenir. All she wanted was to sell some trinkets to sustain her small family another day.' This experience deepened my newly found sense of solidarity with other women. I think I 'knew' how she must have felt.

When I lifted my camera she turned away.
The baby on her back dozed trustingly,
While the daughter of five sold me a pompom bird.
I learned <u>respect and solidarity</u> that day.

29

MOTHER OF US ALL

One summer I visited in Warwick, N.Y. at Pacem in Terris, an 'oasis of inwardness' built by Frederick Franck in honor of Pope John XXIII, whom he described as 'more than a Pope; a very great human being. He is a genius of the heart, the most compelling human, living sign of hope in the desert of this appalling century of man's inhumanity to humanity.'

I was touched deeply by many of his sculptures, his praying in stone, steel and wood. One that was especially meaningful to me was of wood, standing about eight feet tall. This is the image I write about here.

It seemed carved out of a huge tree trunk, and showed a very feminine face looking compassionately upon the people she enfolded in her ever-protective mantle. Franck said to me as he urged me not to miss it, "I call her the Mother of us all." In another place he referred to a similar cosmic face as depicting what Buddhist scriptures teach:

ABSOLUTE WISDOM IS ABSOLUTE COMPASSION AND
ABSOLUTE COMPASSION IS ABSOLUTE WISDOM.

The image and his description of it came so strongly into my prayer during my first visit to Sophia House of Prayer in Milwaukee, Wisconsin, that some of my prayer became the forming of a similar image in clay, and then trying to draw it to share with all the women who are searching for an image of the God who mothers us all: SOPHIA. Not only does she enfold us in her protective mantle of compassion and wisdom; she is clothed in us. We are her robe, her mantle. Through us her wisdom and compassion can be touched, if we but open our hearts and seek to 'see as God sees,' (my favorite description of wisdom.)

We can help to heal the wounds we come upon in our daily lives. We can suffer-with (compassion-ate) those who suffer. Is this the fire that Jesus came to cast upon the earth, that it might be enkindled? He knew intuitively that power had gone out from him when the woman touched his cloak.

Franck also said of Pope John XXIII: "He spoke words of humanity, of compassion, tolerance and peace. Creative words of real wisdom; so exceptional to come from the mouth of the world's great."

MOTHER OF US ALL

The world's great, the world's small
For Sophia it matters not.
Mother of us all,
She clothes us in herself.

Marianne McGriffin, S.P.

SPIRITUAL SEA

One of the first books on my reading list for the Shalem Institute for Spiritual Formation was Tilden Edward's <u>SPIRITUAL FRIEND.</u> I found the first chapter, 'The Spiritual Sea in Which We Swim Today,' very difficult to read. One way I tried to fathom the meaning and implications of the words was to take a piece of clay and handle it while I mulled over the words of the chapter. Some of the thoughts are indicated here, as well as a picture of the piece itself.

As the piece began to take shape, I wanted to show the pounding waves and the fearful thrashing beast. Later, I realized the piece had two sides, one showing the wild waves. On the other side a mouth gapes to swallow while it also draws us toward it. However, the devouring mouth as shown in the clay seems to be the center of a beautiful flower. There is a terrible beauty in the struggle we make to survive and yet to respond to the call of the God who overwhelms us.

THE SPIRITUAL SEA

Open and receiving, thrashing and devouring,
Mystery of our call and resistance, our response and our fear.
This is the new creation of Life and Love and Eternity.
I must step out into God!
God is the vast ocean of love breaking waves over all.
God's tides cannot be anticipated.
God's ways cannot be predicted.
In my imaging, I stand by the Sea,
My back to the inlet formed by huge boulders.
I invite God (the Sea) to come for me.
The sea only laps at my feet.
I become aware of the presence of God not only in the Sea,
But in the sand and the boulders, too.
God is in the beach beneath my feet.
God is in the mountain of stone that surrounds me.
God is in the small expanse of creeping tide that laps at my feet.
God is in the vast ocean which will soon come crashing into the gap in the boulders
Filling it with powerful, rolling waters.
And God is in me as I stand here looking for, waiting for God.

WAITING BY THE SPIRITUAL SEA

Marianne McGriffin, S.P.

TOUCHSTONE IMAGE

This piece of clay became for me a touchstone image for not only my seeking God, but also my accompanying individuals in their journeys. In it, the boulders are huge in the background, but a cave has evolved, before which one figure sits in quiet prayerful reflection while the other searches for words in which to verify his or her own spiritual experience. This image sits on the prayer table between our two chairs during spiritual direction visits.

TOUCHSTONE IMAGE

And so we sit,
you and I.
While you search for your God,
I invite God to come. And wait.

A C O A

A WORKSHOP WAS OFFERED IN South Bend for ministers and church workers. Sister Fran and I went to find out something about ADULT CHILDREN OF ALCOHOLICS, to see if we could learn something that might be helpful in our work with members of the church where we served as Coordinators of Adult and Children's Faith Development. I learned that ACOA is one of those ANONYMOUS groups that have been developed to help persons who grew up with an alcoholic parent, to deal with the coping habits developed over time. While these habits may have been useful in my development some of them are no longer appropriate for an adult. I also learned that the second A in the acronym can stand for almost ANYTHING that affected the entire family's functioning. It could be an overly zealous religiosity, an invalid in the family who claimed much of the parents' attention, extreme poverty, violence frequently experienced in the home or some other abnormality. At this workshop I learned the speaker was not only talking about somebody else, but about me, too. Later I chose to go to a meeting of ACOA to see if I could learn something that would help me in my personal development. That night is described here:

OF COURSE

"Of course I can do that!" I woke up suddenly with these words echoing in my consciousness. What had I been dreaming? I did not know, but I did know what had happened the evening before. It was my first ACOA meeting. A man had just finished talking, his voice and eyes overflowing with tears. My heart was reaching out to him—wanting to let him know that I cared—and before I could say anything to him, someone began her sharing—of HER pain from the past.

I could barely contain myself. How could she be so unfeeling—so self centered as to just go right ahead with what she wanted to say, without even offering him a word of comfort and care? When she finished (I had hardly heard a word she said) I quickly broke in with an effort to let him know my care and concern. It was then I learned the purpose and procedure for an ACOA meeting. We come for OUR sake, not to take care of anyone else, not to give advice, but to allow others' stories to touch the buried memories in our own psyches, and facilitate our movement toward recovery, re-feeling our own lives.

I was grateful for the silence of my companion as we drove the half-hour ride home that night. I was not at all sure I would ever return, and my thoughts and feelings were roiling in massive confusion. However, something deep inside was at peace, and deep sleep came sooner that night than I expected. The sudden arousal with those words, "Of course I can do that!" settled it. I WOULD go back. And I would learn to listen with my heart, and allow myself to FEEL the feelings triggered by another's story. As time went by I even learned to put those feelings into words as I shared my own accounts of long forgotten suppressed experiences. Some time later, with clay in my hands during retreat I experienced the change that was beginning to transpire within me.

Marianne McGriffin, S.P.

BURGEONING TRUST

There is a longing in my heart, a lonely sadness begging forgiveness.
The meanness of anger and revenge softened to regret,
As slowly, slowly the anxious tension of fear and suspicion
Gave way to waving tendrils of gentleness,
Tentative groping for openness and courage.
From hard cold boulders of distrust
Worn down by insistent waves of desire and determination,
The image of trust began to emerge in the clay
As my hands patiently, gently searched out
a smooth forehead, then a benign smile.
Clear confident eyes looked out in a direct gaze, windowing the deliberate honest courage
That welled up from inner depths.
Confidence sounded out like a yodel cast into the valley
That echoes back, clear as a bell.
There is a trusting in my heart now, as present and elusive as
Lily-of-the-Valley-fragrance in springtime.
(J.9.86)

THE OPEN SIDED PITCHER

"Give me a symbol for trust," I whispered into the ear of the clay,
And so she did, at first a simple vessel,
A bowl that was lower on one
side so that it could be filled
Up to a certain level, and then
Whatever is in it would spill out the open side.. A vessel to be filled and emptied, but then it
kept on going, longer and narrower on one end, as it became a pitcher
With handle and spout, and an open side.

REFLECTION

This pitcher cannot be filled with any THING. NO THING can be contained, held in reserve, saved. What comes in goes out. Only God can fill the pitcher and flow out at the same time. The pitcher can be immersed in water; filled in that way, but it cannot be lifted out of the water and remain full. It is open-sided.

IMAGING

I am a vessel, a beautiful whole complete vessel. There is a power, a gentle power called love that calls me to come. I am free to come or not. I am a vessel, an open sided pitcher, whole and complete. Open-sided is the way I am made so as not to be able to hold any THING, only to be a VESSEL for the Spirit of Love to fill and be poured out of, a vessel symbolic of trust. Trust is like that. TRUST is an open sided pitcher. What good is an open sided pitcher? What fills an open sided pitcher?
SPIRIT   SMOKE   AROMA   ESSENCE   AIR   GOD   LOVE   MERCY
JUSTICE   WIND   TRUST

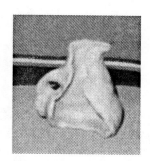

OPEN-SIDED PITCHER

TWELVE STEPS TO TRUST

Give up control, they say,
And I worry and strain and seek to make it happen.

Give up control, they suggest,
And I ask for the grace to let go and let God be God.
Give up control, they keep on saying,
And I begin to look for the missing piece.

Give up control, again!
And I say, yes, I do want to make myself free.
Give up control, they repeat,
And I seek refuge in those who people my past.

Give up control, they reiterate,
And I determine to square it all away.
Give up control, they continue to urge,
And I stand firm in my determination to make all things right.

"Give up control," continues to hound me,
And in desperation, I turn to God.
Show me TRUST, I plead, and slowly
Inexplicably, my clay becomes an open sided vessel.
Unable to hold anything in reserve. Empty.
Overshadowed and immersed in the Spirit of God.
Full.
THE GLORIOUS IMPOSSIBLE!

Marianne McGriffin, S.P.

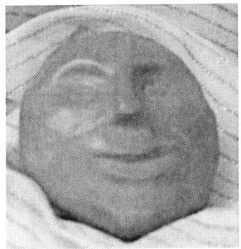

BURGEONING TRUST

SAD MEMORIES

One day I talked with a friend about sadness and depression and the noise in my head.
She suggested I image the sadness.

SAD MEMORIES

I prayed with the clay today,
made many little figures to signify sad memories,
And put them into a small bowl.

I made a Resurrection pall and covered them over
As if they were to be buried.

That didn't seem quite right.
I shaped the pall into a head and face,
Representing the underlying sadness in me.
I had the face crying, with tears running down the cheeks.

I spent some time just sitting
with this sad little girl.

I didn't really want to keep her sad, or to bury her
So I placed her in the loving heart of Jesus,
Wrapped her in God's love.

Then I was able to wipe away the tears, and as I did so,
The whole face seemed happier.
She ended up with a little smile in her eyes and lips.

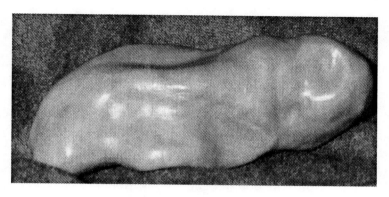

THE SHAPE OF SADNESS

It's like a long drawn-out tear, solidified to last a life-time.
Layers and layers of sadness have been added
One on top of another before the first one was ever shed.
More and more tears have run down and hardened, solidified
Because never really cried;
Formed inside but never allowed to flow freely.

So hardened into a facial expression of stoicism or resistance or determination
Sometimes checked in a silent howl of rage and frustration.

Just as it takes eons to wear down granite into sand,
So will it take a lifetime to change this solidified tear into dust.
Yes. Dust. It is a dry tear.
Only the water of tender compassion can make clay of the dust,
To be used to open someone's eyes,
Making it possible for them not only to see, but also to cry real tears.

Marianne McGriffin, S.P.

TRUTH WILL OUT

In my dreams nothing can be buried,
Hidden in illusion.
Truth will out!

Face to face reality is mirrored
As on the surface of a deep well.
The hurt I have caused cannot be buried forever.
An honest look
Into the countenance of my dream
Is often an unmistakable
Slap in the face.

Truth will out!

CLAY MIRROR

I look into the clay and cannot deceive.
It is the mirror of truth.

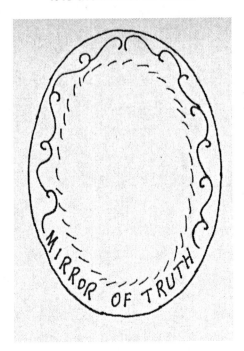

INNER CHILD

For several years beginning in 1980 I used the methods of liberating my inner self, presented by Lucia Cappachione in her workshops and book entitled *RECOVERY OF YOUR INNER CHILD*. My first attempt at finding my inner child in clay came from a dream in which I meet a weeping child. I ask her why she is crying. She looks up and says simply, "Because it hurts!" This weeping child who looks up with some hope in her eyes was one of two pieces of all that I have made so far, which broke in the firing. The logical reason for this is that an air bubble in the thick piece exploded, and split the clay open. I found the break very symbolic. I thought, "Yes, my BROKEN CHILD."

Sometime later I wanted to make a "Happy Child," but she still wasn't there. The best I could do was a "Happy Little Curl."

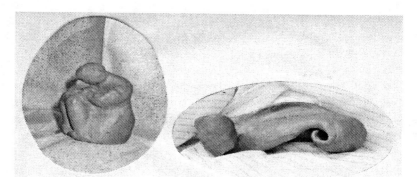

THE BROKEN CHILD and the HAPPY LITTLE CURL

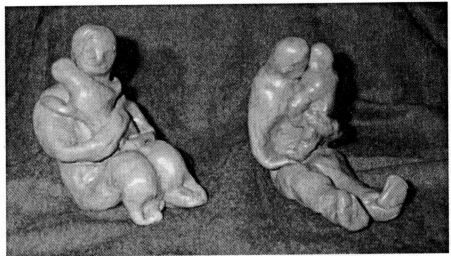

INNER CHILD RECONCILIATION

Then years later, after much inner work and processing, the two figurines of child embracing mother and father seemed to bring some closure to the experiences. These figures signify not only my reconciliation with my deceased father and mother, but also the reconciliation of the child in me with the psychic father/mother within me.

BIRD OF PARADISE

IMAGE

I am a little girl on the farm in Odon. My grandmother and I are walking across the field and we come to some woods. I want to go on into the woods. It seems light and safe. Grandmother agrees and I go on ahead into the woods. I walk along noting the flowers and the trees along the wide path. Soon I see a brilliantly colored bird walking on the path.

It is a huge bird with golden feathers and bright jewel-like tips on the feathers. It turns to look at me and then moves on slowly as if it wants me to follow it. I do walk along behind it admiring all along its beautiful feathers. The bird stops and its feathers fan out like a peacock's, only where the body of the bird is, it is open, like an arch big enough for me to walk through.

I turn to look to my grandmother, and she, far in the distance, nods to go ahead. I enter the archway and find just inside a little stairway up and over a fence. I climb the steps up one side and down the other and find myself in an open field. Here I am on my own. I can no longer see my grandmother, and the bird has disappeared.

I walk slowly, carefully across the field, knowing that every place I put my feet, the grass bends down under my step. I am aware of my steps and the grass and the birds and insects that seem to open up a way for me to go. I come to an ANCIENT WOMAN sitting amidst her pots, turning and pinching one in her hands. I stop and gaze at her for a while.

She pays no heed to me, but continues what she is doing, totally absorbed in the formation of the pot. I see her as a truly contemplative woman. As she works, the bowl become bigger and bigger until it is large enough to contain a person. She looks up at me and back at the bowl as if to invite me to enter into the bowl. She holds it on its side, so I can climb in easily, and as I get in, she turns it up so I can sit comfortably in the bottom of the bowl. The rim at the top is smaller than the bottom, so that when I look up, I can see only a small circle of light.

I had just settled in and become comfortable noticing how the bowl just fits me and is quiet and peaceful, when the POTTER WOMAN stands up to a huge size and picks me up, bowl and all, and with a mighty strength hurls me into space. I feel myself spinning at lightning speed through the air and then I feel myself falling. I hear a huge splash and I know I am now in the midst of a huge ocean. I wonder if I will sink to the bottom, but it seems I am bobbing along on top, moved by the waves, nudged by the fish, and otherwise totally alone.

As I begin to wonder where I am going, what I am doing, I begin to feel a rush of movement and feel myself inside the bowl being drawn along with the current of water into a narrow opening that leads into an underground passageway. I feel myself to be in familiar territory now, in the passageway inside the mountain on which my log cabin is built.

When the bowl bumps against a side of the stream, I quickly disembark, and climb up the stairs I find nearby. I climb higher and higher until I come out in the cabin where SRD is waiting. The workman who is my guardian and my animus stands nearby, also waiting. We have a grand reunion, and I promise to come here more often, of my own accord, not waiting to be sent here by the loving POTTER WOMAN, or the golden bird, or even my grandmother.

During all this time, since I left my grandmother at the edge of the forest, I have grown, and have become mature and whole and trusting. And I have discovered all these ways of entering into union with my God, becoming one in every sense of the word. (J.8.1.85)

Marianne McGriffin, S.P.

REFLECTIONS

(Note from Maria von Franz—*Interpretation of Fairy Tales, p. 6, about the story of Prince Ring:*)

> "When the hero (heroine) is set adrift in a cask, the cask is the vessel that sustains him (her) upon the waters, and in this aspect is motherly and protective; moreover, it allows the water currents to bear him (her) to the intended place."

(For me, the passage is to the interior of the mountain and thence up to the Cabin where Sophia and Po live. These are my inner guides. In my early childhood, I spent much time on my grandmother's farm in Odon, Indiana. I remember her as a loving caring person, who treated me with respect. The POTTER WOMAN in the image represents Sister RoseAnn Trzil, who was my spiritual director for several years, and who introduced me to imaging as a form of prayer. SRD (Sister Rose Dolores) in the image was my spiritual director for the first twenty-five years of my religious life. She used the image of the Dove of the Trinity to help me realize the indwelling of the Trinity in each of us. The Bird of Paradise in the image refers to this image. PO is the name I had given in earlier images to the masculine spirit in me I see as my animus.

I spent many clay times reflecting on this image, and these are the pieces resulting from those times of contemplation.)

BIRD OF PARADISE THROUGH WHOSE GATEWAY I ENTER THE FIELD OF CONTEMPLATION

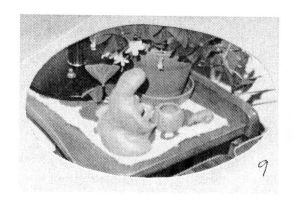

THE POTTER WOMAN
INVITES ME TO
ENTER CONTEMPLATION.

CONTEMPLATION BOWL
IN WHICH I REST IN GOD
IN TRUTH AND IN TRUST.

Marianne McGriffin, S.P.

HOLY WEEK TRIDUUM

During Holy Week of 1998 I followed the suggestion I found in an article in *PRAYING* MAGAZINE #83, entitled *"Sharing the Crucifixion."*

I took my clay with me to <u>Mary's Solitude</u> on the campus of St. Mary's College in South Bend, IN. I spent the three days in retreat, participating in the liturgies in the Sisters' chapel. Each day I prayed the theme of the day with clay in my hands. Some inspiration came from the liturgy itself in the chapel, and more came from readings and reflections during each day.

On HOLY THURSDAY, the line, "Go and prepare the table for the Lord's Supper," led me to do just that in clay, with the words engraved on the edge of the table, with the cup and plate there in readiness.

On GOOD FRIDAY the words I found in a reflection booklet, LIVING FAITH, caught my spirit. The cross is thick and sturdy, and the corpus contorted in pain, but also in JESUS turning his head to breathe out his Spirit and direct the flow of his breath by turning his hand up from the confining nail. "HE HANDED OVER HIS SPIRIT."

SATURDAY was an empty day, with no evidence of Jesus' having even lived, except the soldiers who stand guard over the sealed tomb.

EASTER SUNDAY dawned glorious and alive with the Spirit of the resurrection. The words still echoed: "HE HANDED OVER HIS SPIRIT."

Now I added the words, 'to us!" We must allow the Spirit of Jesus free reign in our hearts and in the world today.

SOLEMN PREPARATION
THURSDAY
**Solemn preparation
Of table for the Lord's Supper,
Of feet, to walk the way,
Of bread and wine, to nourish the new life.**

**He hands over His Spirit to them,
To us all, to live his life now.**

Marianne McGriffin, S.P.

FRIDAY

CONSUMMATION

EXECUTION

DELIVERANCE

**The veil of the temple is ripped away.
The naked body, torn, bleeding, empty,
Is laid to rest, closed in, guarded
Against escape or theft.**

**JESUS
DIVINE. HUMAN.
LIVING. CARING. LOVING.
HANDS OVER HIS SPIRIT.
CHRIST!**

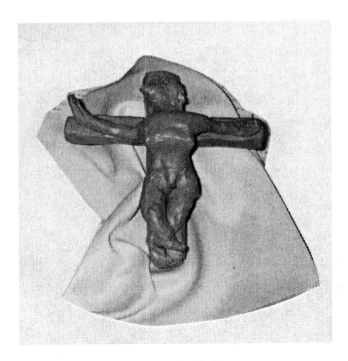

CONSUMMATION

SATURDAY

Emptiness.
God is dead.
Our lives have no meaning.
Until we remember
He said
He would rise again.
Out there, yes, after three days;
But here also, in our hearts.

ABSENCE

Marianne McGriffin, S.P.

SUNDAY

Darkness gives way to brilliance.
The light of Christ shines.
His spirit lives.
His way is our way.
His truth is ours.
His Life-Spirit is in us.

HE HANDED OVER HIS SPIRIT.
ALLELUIA!
TO US.
ALLELUIA!
TO BE OUR ENTHUSIASM,
OUR IN-SPIRATION (IN-BREATHING)
ALLELUIA!
AMEN.

ALLELUIA!

CHAPTER 5

SEE WHAT HAPPENED?

Each person's experience of praying with clay is unique. Some have shared their experiences in writing for inclusion in this book. These accounts follow, and speak for themselves

A HEALING DEEPER THAN PHYSICAL PAIN

For a little over three and a half years I lived with severe pain caused by my jaw joints. Often I had a severe headache. Sometimes the pain incapacitated me.

I felt alienated from God. Where was God in the midst of all this? I'd been an extrovert and suddenly I was an introvert. I'd experienced Christ through other people, but many people found it hard to be with someone in pain all the time. I didn't know how to explain the pain. It affected my emotional, spiritual and relational self. I was much more vulnerable emotionally. Barriers that I had put up to block out pain suddenly weren't as strong in maintaining my emotional equilibrium.

Spiritually, I found out that I didn't have a very good view of God. I had a hard time praying to God. My physical pain very much affected how I saw God. Just as I went to a doctor to get help for my physical pain I found it very important to have a spiritual mentor from whom to get help in seeing how God was working in my life. I didn't feel like God was there. My vision of God was very much clouded by pain.

During that time I went on a retreat led by a Catholic Sister. The retreat was called <u>Praying with Clay.</u> Sister Marianne gave us a lump of clay and talked about how God created us. You are also creators, she said, and God can use your hands to speak. We were supposed to just work with the clay, giving some shape to the hurt inside us. So I began to work with the clay. What came out was a little girl. She was all bundled up, still, and maybe scared. Through this work of my hands I was able to pray! It was a very healing experience. Praying with clay, it seemed, allowed God to bring to light anything. I didn't have to put word to pain.

Another figure I worked on I called Horror. This one, a kind of horror face, represented my physical pain. I couldn't understand why I had to suffer like this. At the same time there didn't seem to be any end to it. Sometimes people would say, *'Oh, there's a light at the end of the tunnel.'* I felt that light was a train coming at me a hundred miles an hour.

As I was working with the clay another time, I started to see a back. It was the back of a person. I thought, 'That's *me in the midst of my pain, all alone.'* But then I started seeing another back. I thought, *'Oh, that first back was God. And this one that isn't very well formed is me.'* I felt pulled between God and the pain, yet it was an important moment for me. For the first time I saw God in my pain. I'd felt alone for so long.

51

A third figure dealing with my physical pain I called wrestling. I'd been doing some imaging with Marlene Kropf, of Jacob wrestling with God. I felt like I was wrestling with my pain. But my pain was also God. The pain was always bigger than I was and it was an intense battle. And it hurt. Even in the rare days when I was larger than my pain I still had certain scars from the pain, things that I'll always carry with me.

I realized how much I needed to pray to God about my struggle. Yet it's so easy to get caught up in the struggle and feel God is way out there that you don't talk to God about it.

A fourth figure represents another aspect of my spiritual journey.

The figure doesn't really have a name.

"HERE I AM"

A phrase kept going through my head when I worked on it: *'Here I am.'* In the clay figure I was screaming out to God that I needed help. I was also screaming out to other people that I needed help, that I couldn't handle the long journey anymore. I really needed help. With my hands I shaped a prayer for help. One answer came in the form of self-acceptance of here I am with pain and all.

In the fifth figure I'm standing. Sometimes you think that healing comes in a moment. For me, that healing process took a little over a year. I had to work through a lot of things. So when I was working on this figure I very much felt like, *'Okay, I'm going to stand.'*

When I showed the figure to other people they immediately said, *'It looks like you have a heavy load on your back.'* I realized how important community is in bringing things to life for me, to help me embrace the pain. I didn't need to grit my teeth and stand up with all my power. When I finally stood up, I felt like something had closed, that some healing process had happened. The healing focused on a spiritual and emotional health. I felt that spiritual, emotional and physical health are so tied together that if you are hurting in one area you are probably weak in another because it has worn you down.

My last figure seems to be completely different from the others. God is comforting me. Before, I always felt like you've got to give up your problems. You're calling up, trying to get God's attention, but never sure that you have it. I realized that's not right for me. I need to go sit in God's lap and get comfort and cry and tell God what's the problem. I have a totally different image of God. Now. To me that has broadened my understanding of God and how God relates to us.

(Brenda Glanzer Lilliston, of Wichita, Kansas.)

Here is another first hand account of how praying with clay helped a woman move through a painful period in her life.

LISTENING TO THE VOICE OF GODDE

The first time I held the cold red clay in my hands, I was still trying to figure out if GODDE could really use me for ministry. I was not new to the Seminary. It was my third semester of study. But GODDE spoke to me. As I worked the clay, I became transfixed by the breaking of it, how smooth it was on the outside, and yet how it snapped and broke so easily. Out of that experience came a broken wing, symbolizing for me the beginning of my own healing, and a true conviction that GODDE could indeed use my own woundedness in ministering to others.

About a year later, I would return to the clay after a serious hospitalization, and time spent on the critical list. We had been praying Scripture verses, and I chose Psalm 131. A figure of a mother holding a toddler to her breast came out. GODDE was again speaking to me, telling me I would always have a place to be helped and loved and cared for, no matter what. It was then that I realized that the clay could give incredible voice to GODDE in our relationship, as well as hold the possibility of freeing my own scared voice within.

Several months later, I would begin my own steady journey with the clay. It was through the clay that I could find expression for those things for which I couldn't find words. Each piece I did had it's own story, its own message, and it varied between people who saw the pieces. But each piece also has its own life.

Soon after I began working with the clay on a steady basis, Sister Marianne challenged me to fire them instead of just allowing them to air dry. I lost those first two pieces. The wing was shattered into a million pieces in the kiln, and the mother and child broke into a variety of large and small pieces. I was able to reassemble most of the mother and child. That, too, had a lesson for me. I was growing, and I had to look at where I was, and whether or not I was ready to move on. The journey to the kiln is long and thoughtful for me. For each piece, the time frame is different. Some pieces I run to be fired as soon as they are dry enough. But others, I just can't emotionally release yet, so they remain in a dry/not - fired state. Since that first time, however, I have not lost any pieces in the firing process.

But the clay...the clay for me holds incredible power, and empowerment. It allows me first of all to listen to GODDE. It also allows me to talk to GODDE in a non-verbal way. For most of us, non-verbal communication is difficult. But this form of communication is personal and goes way beyond the moment of formation. (Learning to listen to the clay can be difficult, as I can get my own creative ideas, but it does happen.) I also journal after completing every piece, but I am often able to go back and reflect or journal on a piece weeks or months later. The pieces are not stale. They hold GODDE'S voice.

The clay puts me in touch with a GODDE who formed this world we call earth. Working it gives me a creative power similar to that of my own

Marianne McGriffin, S.P.

Creator. It is personal, and it always speaks to me where I am. It is through the clay that I can find GODDE'S voice if I am willing to listen.

(Judith Guasch, a student at American Mennonite Biblical Seminaries in Elkhart, IN, 1999, used with permission.)

TRANSFORMATION MIRRORED IN CLAY

When something momentous happens in our lives, we often remember the place where it occurred in vivid detail. Who would have known that there in that tiny, dark little 'MEDITATION ROOM' at St. Vincent's parish in 1986, I would begin a journey, an intense, sometimes frightening, sometimes ecstatic journey, into those parts of myself that had been submerged for so long? I will never forget the excitement and zeal with which my co-worker, Sister Marianne, returned from a workshop/retreat in the west on praying with clay. Later, in that little meditation room, using focusing prayer as outlined by Edwin McMahon, Peter Campbell and Eugene Gendlin, Sister Marianne encouraged me to sculpt the images that came to me in prayer.

Somehow, as I sculpted these small pieces, which started out pretty frightening, and gradually became more joyful, I was able to record in clay this process of life-altering transformation. Moreover, the actual physical manipulation of these clay figures turned out to be quite therapeutic and to lead me along the path toward healing and wholeness. For example, initially the only image that came to me in prayer was that of a 'Humpty-Dumpty' type figure that was stuck between the folds of my inner self. In my imagination I would use a hook to try to pull the little creature out. I formed the image in clay, along with a hook that was separate from the figure, but which fit into a notch in its back. I could physically pull at the image, and believe that somehow this may have loosened up the inner Humpty-Dumpty, for after several sessions I was able to pull the sad little thing out, and it changed to a new figure, that of a little girl crying with her head against the wall. Again, I formed her image in clay, and tried to comfort her and massage her back. I did this for several weeks before the little girl within me felt safe enough to turn to me in my prayer and begin to tell something of her story; of her frustrations, and feeling of desperation.

Over a period of close to fourteen years, I have 'journaled' my inner prayer experience in clay. Most often, what emerges from the clay is totally spontaneous, and may take time to understand. Mirrored in my clay pieces are hopes, frustrations, gifts, messages, and appeals to open my eyes, ears, and heart. (Jane Cors Smith, of Mishawaka, Indiana.)

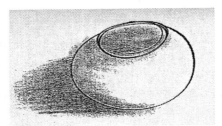

BOWL

CLAY, THE MAGIC; GOD THE MAGICIAN

Clay, you bewitch; you transform; you are magic. I hold a clay ball, gently caressing it between open palm, my hands yearning to squeeze, pummel, and sculpt a dragon of anger and fire. Transfigured, altered clay, you do not speak. Always you acquiesce to the magician, the God, who through the potter, gives birth to illuminated archetypes, unconscious images from the psyche.

A nest for containment, a bird with twisted neck, an ambivalent cat, a woman with no face, all sit on a shelf reminding me of my evolving journey of prayer with clay. Figures wrought through determination, tears, spirit, and vitality are indeed sacred.

"Moderation, my dear, moderation!"

There is no moderation working spontaneously with clay; no withholding energy, just exuding raw emotion. Where is the moderation in the universe, in the orgasmic thrust of creation or in the icon of cross, thorns and nails? Where is the moderation when we are born and our cries are heard for the first time?

It is the Magician's clay that I need for healing murderous impulses, grief, and passion. It is the Magician's clay that allows the inner child full reign, full throttle. It is clay that says nothing, but is silence, holds everything. It is the Magician, however, who crowns creativity and spirituality as one.

(Ellen Schmidt, of Granger, Indiana, May, 2002)

GENESIS IN CLAY

Dear Lord of the Universe,
I touch the cold clay,
Fingers grasping the hard mass.
Instantly, I am close to you.
What flashed through your infinite BEING as you fashioned the world?
Were your eyes closed in concentration as mine were today?
Did you play?
Squeeze, twist, poke holes
In the earth mass at first?
I DID.
Was the beginning of creation
Fun for you?
Ah, I thought so.
Lord, you are the genius,
Creating the supreme masterpiece
In seven days.
While I struggled
Ending up with what few would
Recognize
But You and I know my images,
Don't we?
My human form's pretty good
But I couldn't shape you.
How dare I even try?
Then my inner eyes
Found the representative image,
A rock. Indented in the middle,
Where I can hide
Sheltered, communicating with you
A space to gather my courage Lord, hear my cry
See me doubled over in supplication
Help me heal the hole in my heart
Bless me as I claim my mission
Once more.

(Joyce Bruckner, used with permission.)

CHAPTER 6

CENTERING A POT/INTEGRATING A LIFE

In centering we have to be passionate.
We must be able to BE.
We must BE Open SPaces
And let the winds of life blow through us,
To breathe with the winds,
To bend with the winds,
To stand upright,
To be intact.
To be persons.

BE ATTUNED TO THIS DIALOGUE
OF THE VISIBLE AND THE INVISIBLE.
(Helen of Atchison)

No book on praying with clay is complete without a chapter on making pots on a wheel, even thought the main focus is on prayer as SCULPTING with clay. Throwing the pot on the wheel can be a very centering experience for the potter. BEING the pot that is thrown has its parallels with the turning points of our lives. Praying, pot making and contemplation have much in common. Thomas Keating's statement about unconscious material seems to support this relationship.

> *"Our unconscious contains all the emotional trauma of a lifetime that we have repressed as well as enormous levels of energy and creativity. Every significant event of our life history is recorded in our bodies and nervous systems. The undigested emotional material of a lifetime must be moved out in order for the free flow of grace and the natural and spiritual energies in the unconscious to manifest." (Thomas Keating, OSCO in "Contemplative Outreach News" Vol. 13 # 1 July, 1999.)*

It seems to me that this 'moving out' of undigested emotional material is facilitated by the total involvement of the potter in the making of the pot. Before I ever was introduced into praying with clay as I do it now, I had spent a sabbatical year throwing pots on a wheel in the OLD FIELD HOUSE at Notre Dame in the year 1979-1980. I had spent almost every afternoon making pots and experiencing the healing effects of centering the clay on the wheel. I now describe that process in this way:

I see the making of a bowl, and the story of a life as parallel. If the bowl IS my life, the time I spend now is to re-enter the bowl and integrate the various traumas of my formation.

Spiraling in, spiraling out:
Design upon the wheel of life
Signals workings of potter and clay.
Tearing down and building up
Pressing in and pressing out,
Yielding and resisting,
Centering of Potter and Clay

CENTERING:

The bowl, pot, vessel is formed from a rounded mass of clay that has been thrown very hard onto a turning wheel. The potter's whole body, mind, heart and soul is exercised in centering the mass of clay, with hand pressure evenly bestowed on the clay as it turns on the wheel. As the mound becomes balanced and centered, the potter's body begins to feel at-one with the clay and the process. This reminds me of how deeply God the Potter is continuously involved in my formation. It also reminds me of the struggle I the clay experience in the evolvement of my BEING.

SHAPING:

Now that the clay is whole and centered it is pressured in a different way. The potter's thumbs begin to penetrate at the top of the mound. All the while the pressure from outside continues. As the well at the top deepens, the sides must rise to accommodate the open space being formed.

The potter knows the depths to which she can take the crater. When that depth is reached, not too far, but far enough to allow a solid base, the life-time pressures move up the sides of the bowl, constantly raising and pressing, pulling up and pressing, inside and out. Occasionally the top rim is leveled to keep it strong and even.

I, the clay must begin sooner or later to cooperate with the creator. I shift, accept, resist, and respond. While being raised up with the pressure from inside and out I reach up and out and hold fast to my very substance. As the pressures subtly effect new shape I remember, and remember again and the bowl takes on the shape toward which it is called. Even when it reaches its potential shape and size, it is still not finished.

SEPARATION

The pot must be removed from the wheel, a separation which can be disastrous or life-giving. Assuming the bowl is not destroyed in the separation process, it is set aside and allowed to dry slowly.

I see myself as holding on to who I have become and letting go of all that holds me down. In the drying time I regain strength while resting, breathing in, breathing out.

TRIMMING

When dry but not too dry to allow for refinement, it is trimmed, at the top if necessary; at the bottom to better define the base on which it stands. The MARK OF THE MAKER is firmly carved into the base of the bowl. *Parallel movement in my life encourages me to divest, decide, take a stance.*

FIRING

In the firing, moisture and air are consumed, leaving only the stone skeleton of the bowl. It is now naked, rocklike, and pristinely WHAT IT IS. But it is still not finished. *The time of firing may be any hardship in life. Whatever it is, it purifies and firms up. It is in these times I explore and discover the fires of passionate living.*

ADORNMENT

The potter creates colors and designs uniquely fitted to this particular pot-bowl. The pot receives these as welcome cover for its barrenness. Just as it begins to 'feel pretty' the pot is subjected to another firing. Once more deliberately placed in the furnace, the pot is purified again, this time to set in place the design of the Maker, and the BEAUTY OF THE BOWL. *I choose the gifts of God. I acknowledge and become one with the BEAUTY bestowed both within and without.*

PURPOSE

The pot may be placed on a stand for all to enjoy, or put to some very practical use, but *however God chooses to treat me I use and share the gifts of God.*

At the end of the year of centering, healing and reflecting on the above processes, I wrote the following:

A HANDFUL OF DUST

God picked up a handful of dust and gazed at it with unlimited love. God said, '*You are Marianne*," and set about designing this new creation. God added some water to the very dry dust which had just been called by name. Then God added some divine sweat and blood and tears, and life-giving breath.

God threw the clay onto a turning wheel, the living moving wheel of life and pushed and pulled and patted and caressed her. God pressured her both inside and out; drew her up and out, formed her, shaped her, and they were both satisfied.

Gently God lifted her off, admired her and loved her. God called upon her to rest a while, and placed her gently on a shelf. She waited, and grew strong.

Then God came back and tested her strength and tried her weakness. And God filled her with FIRE, inside and out, making her one with the fire. God enlightened her shadows, drew them into the white-hot heat of Divine Love, She realized her very BEING is in God.

God picked her up, loved her, brushed her gently with a delicate design. God held her close and pressed her once more into the white-hot heat of a loving embrace.

And God said, *"Marianne, I have this GREAT SECRET that I want to share with all the world. Will you help me?"*

Marianne said, *"I will."*

YES IS SUCH A SMALL INSIGNIFICANT WORD TO SAY BUT I SAY IT WITH ALL MY BEING, ALL THAT I AM AND ALL THAT I HAVE.

POT

CENTERING

Each of us has many hungers. But they all seem to be versions of a two-fold one: hunger for freedom and hunger for union, a dance of each individuality with the world. A capacity to yield is strengthened in me, in any potter, as I do not merely use these materials to certain ends. Once my soul is yielded up, the transformations of the clay will speak to me as my own. The inner laws of life seem to me to be simultaneously unique centers, spinning in continuous relation to each other.

Sister Helen Buening OSB of Atchison Kansas, author of this article, working at her wheel.

Marianne McGriffin, S.P.

We are transformed, not by adopting attitudes toward ourselves but by bringing into center all the elements of our sensations and our thinking and our emotions and our will: all the realities of our bodies and our souls, all the dark void in us of our undiscovered selves, all the small light of our discovered being. All the drive of our hungers, and our fairest and darkest dreams; all, all the elements come into center, into union with all other elements. And in such a state they become quite different in function than when they are separated and segregated and discriminated between or against.

When we act out of an inner unity, when all of ourselves is present in what we do, then we can be said to be 'on center.' The clay is a very selfish medium. It asks for total self-giving.

Part of our skill as potters is to use all the clay on the wheel in any given form. Our wholeness as persons is expressed in using all our selves in any given act. In this way the self integrates its capacities into a personal potency, as someone who serves life from the center at every instant. In this way knowledge can become a quality of consciousness and illumine our behavior spontaneously and truthfully. Personal transformation, or the art of becoming a human being, has a very special counterpart in the potter's craft—the art of *Centering.*

(Sister Helen Beuning, OSB, in *"Woman of Earth: Transformation in Clay and Fire,"* in *BENEDICTINES, 1982.)*

A pot is

>*An outside*
>*Thrown + punched + pulled*
>*Fired up with life*
>*Firmed up in the firing*
>*But more...*
>*Wait to be touched*
>*And more...*

A pot is

>*A holy inside—outside*
>*To touch what's inside carefully*
>*To be touched outside in awe*
>*To hold earth-treasures*
>*Flowers + trees + sand + water*
>*To hold nourishing-treasures*
>*Bread + soup + wine + herbs*

A pot is

>*Formed + held + entrusted*
>*With human hands and spirit*
>(M.C.Keene, S. P. for the Potter's house pottery studio,
>Karen Van De Walle, C.S.J., potter)

Marianne McGriffin, S.P.

The following story of the relationship of potter, clay, and life experience comes from a very dear friend who is poet, storyteller and dream-keeper, Martha Bartholomew, of Dundee, IL. She had shared the story with me long before it was published in her book, <u>Tellers of Story, Keepers of Dreams</u>, Bristol, IN, Wyndham Hall Press, 1998, in which she introduces the story with these words: 'Here is a mythic story to be read once, lived with, and read again. What did it mean? What does it mean? What can it come to mean? The interpretation will be as unique as the participant hearer.' Since that publication, Martha has revised the story to read:

THE POTTER'S JAR

Grandmother Ayyalah spoke:
"Opher, as I have drawn the warmth and wisdom of the brown earth that runs deep into the Soul of us all—so now must you, alone. The time of my leaving has come."
With that she reached her hand to trace a tear on the younger woman's cheek—smiled her blessing and closed her eyes for a final time.

****

It was several seasons later when Opher, a potter's apprentice to the older woman, was summoned to her doorway by the Messenger of the Wise and Ancient One of the Far Hills. Word had spread far and wide concerning the Ayyalah's practiced hands. The excellence of her work had been noted by all. Now the younger potter was to be tested—on her own merit.
The Ancient One had already sampled the excellence of her work and the command was that she should make a jar to be presented during a ceremony to be held sometime hence. The jar was to be of certain size; it was to bear precise markings and a glaze of a specific color. It has to be without flaw. She would have the honor of presenting the piece to the Wise and Ancient One in person. A price was agreed upon with the Messenger who left and Opher soon set to work. She gathered clay from several secret sources, as well as from places well known to her people. She wedged the colors and textures with water from a hidden spring. She set aside this preparation and entered into her own with fasting and offerings to the Four Winds and the Six Directions and when the Sun rose on the third morning of the last month before the festival she began to form the jar.
As morning turned and the pot began to grow Raven came, perching on a nearby branch, watching. Presently Raven spoke,
"My sister, why do you make a jar so large? It will be too heavy to carry up the hill from the place of water.'
"Because it has been commanded," she replied, continuing her work without looking up.
After noon Wolf appeared on a nearby hill and howled:
"My friend, why do you labor so hard and so long?'
"Because the clay is moist and speaking to my fingers," she said, continuing to mount coil upon coil, smoothing each round of the rising form.
Hours later The Child walked toward her from across the Desert, from around Rock, to Stand near and say,
"I am hungry."
Opher did not look up, but directed, *"Reach inside my shawl. You may have my bread."*
Raven flew away. Wolf wandered off. The Child gathered sticks to lay a fire before disappearing in the manner of its coming. Sun set, but not before kindling Fire with the last of its rays. There was warmth and Fire and Star and Moonlight as Opher the young potter

continued her task. Finally, the first rays of Sun's return revealed the finest jar she had ever made, built to the prescribed form and bearing markings as detailed by the Messenger.

Opher dipped moss into the spring and wrapped the piece she had made so that it would dry slowly and evenly through the warmth of the day. It stood where it had been formed, sheltered from the direct rays of Sun by an overhang of rock ledge. Opher lay down near her work to sleep—to dream.

****

The Day of the Festival had arrived. In her finest garments, wearing the bracelets and necklaces of her ancestors, she appeared before the Gathering of the Tribes in the Far Hills. From the largest wikiup in the Sacred Circle, at the appointed time, there stepped the Wise and Ancient One who had commissioned her work, that by now had been fired to the assigned color in a pit of buffalo dung. Nearly as tall as she, the Jar was nevertheless light enough, now that it was hard and dry and fired, that she could manage to carry it.

'Raven was right,' she thought. 'This jar will be too heavy to carry if it is filled with water or grain.' Momentarily, she wondered, 'What will it hold?' With the hard work and days of fast behind her now, perhaps, she would soon know from the ancient One, the purpose of the piece she had consented to make. It was wrapped in her blanket that she carefully unwound, slowly revealing the vessel of her dedication.

The Circle of People was quiet, whereas only moments before, there had been dancing and chanting to the beat of Drum.

"Let us be One with the Infinite Sun—Forever and ever—
Let us be One with the Infinite Sun—Forever."

When the last fold fell from Opher the Potter's jar—she knelt—then rose with it in her arms as she stepped forward. The Wise and Ancient One nodded—raised a hand. With this permission, she looked into the lined face that seemed vaguely familiar. She heard a voice she had almost forgotten.

"Very Beautiful!" There was a pause—then the directive came:

"NOW! DROP IT!"

A finger pointed to a slab of stone that lay between where each of them stood.

Opher looked deeply into the eyes that held her gaze—gasped—but quickly knew the answer to the question of her thoughts only a short time ago—'What will it hold?'

Without hesitation she raised the prized Jar to release it into a thousand pieces. Then, without a glance at the broken shards scattered about her feet, and unaware of the thin red line that flowed from a small cut upon her cheek, she received a sign—by gesture—from the hands of the Wise and Ancient One. She turned to survey familiar faces among the people who surrounded her. Slowly, but purposefully, she moved through the Sacred Circle that ringed a pungent fire of sage. She walked with a new understanding:

The contents of her Jar was to be—what it had been—from ancient clay to hidden springs—from questioning creatures to hungry child. Already, it was full of all she had allowed through her while she fashioned this her offering. She knew this is what the Jar would hold—always.

She walked now, head high, eyes straight ahead, to her place in the Wisdom Circle where among others there waited Raven, Wolf and the Child.

It was as Sun rose above the Far Hills, and a new day awakened the Drums resumed for those who dance. They began to move and to chant.

Marianne McGriffin, S.P.

"Now she is One with the Infinite Sun—Forever and Ever."

****

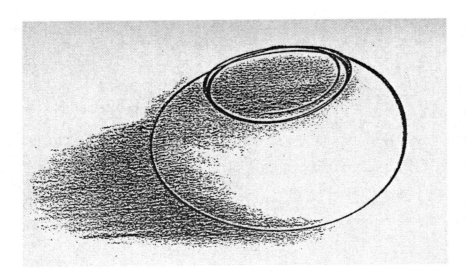

APPENDIX

CLAY

CLAY PASSAGES IN SCRIPTURE

REFLECTIONS ON CREATION STORY IN GENESIS

IMAGING IN PRAYER

RESOURCES USED AND SUGGESTED

·"BLESSED ARE YOU, LORD OUR GOD"

ANNOTATED BIBLIOGRAPHY

TOPICAL INDEX

Marianne McGriffin, S.P.

CLAY

Any type of clay may be used for prayer, natural or synthetic, such as Della Robbia or Plasticene, Sculpey or Play-Doh. However, my favorite is natural clay called INDIAN RED CLAY or simply RED CLAY. It can be fired at cone 05-06. Thicker pieces need to start very low and come up to 05-06.

RECIPE

You can even make your own clay substitute such as you may have made at home for school projects. One recipe is as follows:

COMBINE   2 cups flour
1-cup salt
1 tablespoon powdered alum. (This will keep the clay from souring.)

MIX WITH 1/3-cup water or enough to soften mixture and make it pliable.

COLOR with food coloring or poster paint if you want colored clay.

KNEAD until smooth and usable.

WRAP in a damp cloth and store in a covered container.

REFRIGERATE for longer storage.

If it hardens, sprinkle some water on it and work it in.

Some like to keep each piece of clay they form, as a reminder of the prayer of the time. Others for various reasons simply fold in the shape they have made, and return the clay to the barrel after having used it for prayer and reflection.

Whatever you do with it afterward, just know it's the PROCESS that is most important. Sometimes the PRODUCT serves as a reminder later on, and that's OK.

Marianne McGriffin, S.P.

CLAY PASSAGES IN SCRIPTURE

GENESIS 2:7 *Yahweh God fashioned man from the dust of the soil. Then he breathed into his nostrils a breath of life and thus man became a living being.*

ISAIAH 29:16 *Is the potter no better than the clay? Can something that was made say of its maker, 'He did not make me'? or a pot say of the potter, 'He is a fool'?*

ISAIAH 64:8 *Yet O Lord, you are our father; we the clay and you the potter, we are all the work of your hand.*

JEREMIAH 18:1-5 *The word that was addressed to Jeremiah by the Yahweh, Get up, and make your way to the potter's house: there I shall let you hear what I have to say. So I went down to the potter's house and there he was working at the wheel. And whenever the object of clay which he was making turned out wrong, as happens with the clay handled by potters, he would start afresh and work it into another vessel, as potters do.*

PSALM 103:13-14 *As tenderly as a father treats his children so Yahweh treat those who fear him; he knows what we are made of, he remembers we are dust.*

JOHN 9:6-11 *He spat on the ground, and made a paste of the spittle, Put this over the eyes of the blind man, and said to him, "Go, wash in the pool of Siloam," (a name that means sent.) So the blind man went off and washed himself, and came back with his sight restored.*

WISDOM 15:7 *Take a potter, now, laboriously working the soft earth, shaping all sorts of things for us to use. Out of the same clay, even so, he models vessels intended for clean purposes and the contrary sort, all alike; but which of these two uses each will have is for the potter himself to decide.*

ROMANS 9:20-21 *The pot has no right to say to the potter: 'Why did you make me this shape? 'Surely the potter can do what he likes with the clay? It is surely for him to decide whether he will use a particular lump of clay to make a special pot or an ordinary one?*

2 Corinthians 4:7 *We are only the earthenware jars that hold this treasure, to make it clear that such an overwhelming power comes from God and not from us.*

Marianne McGriffin, S.P.

REFLECTIONS ON THE CREATION STORY
AS ILLUSTRATED BY MICHAELANGELO

Read *Genesis 1:26*

God said, 'Let us make man in our image, in the likeness of ourselves, and let them be masters of the fish of the sea, the birds of heaven, the cattle, all the wild beasts, and all the reptiles that crawl upon the earth.'

Read Genesis 2:7

Yahweh God fashioned man of dust from the soil. Then he breathed into his nostrils a breath of life, and thus man became a living being.

(When I use these passages, I usually paraphrase them to use inclusive language.)

Here are some thoughts from reflections on the painting by Michaelangelo, which Sister Helen Buening used in her introduction to praying with clay:

Look at God—Eve is there in the crook of God's arm. She waits, and all the children to come are behind her, also waiting in amazement at God's wonderful creation.

Notice that God has his arm around Eve, and behind Eve are all of the unborn children of the world. We are included in God's arm reaching out and embracing Eve and all of us who are behind her. Adam, just having been molded and shaped, waits for the life-giving breath, looks not at God, but towards Eve who waits. And Eve looks beyond God and her creation to Adam. The story is of man needing woman to complete the whole.

Adam is stretched out on the total earth, nothing there, just Adam. The Lord has given Adam complete control of all the earth; animals, trees, all these wonderful things. God has made us a little less than the angels. We can use the world for our good. God chose us because of God's love for us. God is always there reaching out.

One of the most beautiful expressions of human art, to know that within one square inch on the left side is lifelessness (the spirit has not yet been placed in Adam) and the powerful hand of God just about ready to close the space, to touch the inanimate piece of clay, let that clay become the image of God because of the spirit that will exist within that individual.

God's hand is poised, motionless. God is in ecstasy at the beauty of the most magnificent of all that has yet been created so that we can become part of creation.

Marianne McGriffin, S.P.

Consider this: the body is born as all things are born, but the spirit, made to the image and likeness of God once created by the Creator will never cease to be.

Here God the Creator has just joined heaven and earth, spirit and flesh, breath and clay in an all-new being. Humanity is made in the IMAGE AND LIKENESS OF GOD.

(Used with Sister Helen's permission)

IMAGING IN PRAYER

The fantasies we use are intended for these purposes:
1. To enable us to know ourselves better.
2. To enable us to love ourselves more truthfully.
3. To enable us to love our neighbor as ourselves.
4. To enable us to expand the use of our capacities for knowing and loving.
5. And hence to make better decisions in our daily living.

Q. Why do we use our imaginations in our prayer?
A. To help us LOVE our selves, our neighbor and our God with greater depth and understanding.

Q. What happens in an IMAGING IN PRAYER SESSION?
* ❖ We share comfortably how things are with us in our everyday lives.
* ❖ We quiet our body and mind, relax, and allow ourselves to deepen our awareness.
* ❖ We put on some soft relaxing music. Guided by our leader, we imagine ourselves in a particular circumstance.
* ❖ In silence, we allow our imaginations to carry us deeper into the experience.

Q. Then what happens?
A. After about 20 minutes the leader calls us back out of the fantasy world into the physical, conscious world. After some moments of silent reflection on our experience we begin to share with the group what our experience was and/or how we now feel as a result of the experience.

Q. Do I HAVE to tell what goes on in my imaginary experience?
A. No. We share only what we are comfortable sharing.

Q. Why do we share at all?
A. Putting into words what is happening to us helps us to be more fully conscious not only of the experience, but of its significance for us. Also, hearing others' experiences can deepen our own faith and prayer life.

Q. What if somebody doesn't agree with what I say, and starts arguing or telling me what I should do?
A. This is a faith-sharing session.
It is NOT A TEACHING OR DISCUSSION SESSION.
The listeners need only hear with respect and reverence what is said. No response is expected or necessary.

Q. What if I share something very personal?

A. **This whole experience IS very personal. Entering into it necessarily implies integrity and respect for one another's personal sharing. Whatever is shared during an IMAGING IN PRAYER session is to be held in the greatest confidence by all participants.**

Q. **Is IMAGING IN PRAYER something I can do alone at home?**

A. **Yes. These are LEARNING SESSIONS in that sense. You can use your imagination in prayer at home in the privacy of your own prayer time and place.**

RESOURCES USED AND SUGGESTED

"ABBA FATHER," by Carey Landrey on album, **ABBA FATHER**, North American Liturgical Resources,2110 West Peoria Ave. Phoenix, AZ 85209 1977.

"EARTHEN VESSELS," NALR.

"FROM EARTHENWARE JARS," by Jack Miffleton.

"GREAT THINGS HAPPEN!" by Carey Landrey, NALR, 1971.

"THE LIGHT SHINES ON," by Carey Landrey on album, **COMPANIONS ON THE JOURNEY,** NALR, 1985.

"LIKE A SEAL ON YOUR HEART," by Carey Landrey, on album, **ABBA FATHER**, NALR 1977.

"ONE BREAD, ONE BODY," by John Foley, New Dawn Music, Inc. 1978

"RAINBOW PATH," BY Kay Gardner, may be obtained from LADYSLIPPER, INC. 3205 Hillsborough Rd. Durham, NC 27705.

"REFLECTIONS," by Adam Martin Geiger of Lura Media. This piece of music is on the reverse side of a tape, "Like a River," included in JOURNEYS TO RENEWAL, a two week renewal program combining music, guided imagery, and journaling, published by LURA MEDIA, 10227 Autumnview Lane, San Diego, CA, 92126-0998,1987.

"WHAT YOU HEAR IN THE DARK," BY Dan Schutte, S.J. NALR, 1987.

"WE ARE MANY PARTS," by Marty Haugen, GIA, 1987.

"YOU ARE NEAR," BY Dan Schutte, S.J., NALR 1973.

Marianne McGriffin, S.P.

BLESSED ARE YOU, LORD OUR GOD,
WHO HAS FILLED CREATION WITH LIGHT AND SPLENDOR

Radiant Lord,
 We rejoice with hearts filled with gratitude
 That You are not a hidden God,
 For You reveal yourself daily
 Through the mystery of light.
Your majesty and glory
 Shine out from within all of creation,
 As well as from sun, moon and stars.
We walk by their light,
 And we also feed upon that light
 As it is transformed daily into our food.

Blessed are you, Illuminator of All Creation,
 For the gifts of sunrise, high noon and sunset.
In the splendor of the sun,
 The sky-wheel of energy and light,
 We see your splendor, O Light of Lights.
Your Son, Jesus, called Himself The light of the world
 And invited us to be His luminous brothers and sisters
 And Your children of light.

We are grateful for the daily light of insight,
 That gift by which we see our way to you.
We are also grateful for shadows and nightfall
 Which serve as background for this light.
In our lives, we often stand
 In darkness of failings and suffering.
May Your Divine Light
 Penetrate the murky overcast of these times,
 And radiate outward from the horizon of our hearts.
May Your Divine Presence
 Be a shining star in the midst of gloom.
Like plants of the earth, may we lean toward you,
 Eternal Source of All Light and Energy,
Help us, this day, to *be* light to all we meet.
 Blessed are You, Lord, our God,
 Who has filled creation with light and splendor. Amen

(Reprinted with permission from PRAYERS FOR THE Domestic Church by Father Edward Hays, copyright Forest of Peace Publishing, Inc. 251 Muncie Rd, Leavenworth KS 66048-4946)

Marianne McGriffin, S.P.

ANNOTATED BIBLIOGRAPHY

ADAMS, JAMES E., Editor, **Living Faith**, Periodical Publications. 10300 Watson Road, St. Louis, MO 63127. (Reflections during Holy Week.)

ANONYMOUS, "*You are a Child of the Universe.*"

BAYLOR, BYRD, **When Clay Sings**, Aladdin Books, Macmillan, New York, 1972 (The daily life and customs of prehistoric southwest Indian tribes are retraced from the design on the remains of their pottery. Poetic, picture book.

BANKSON, Marjory Zoet, **This is MY Body: Creativity, Clay and Change**. Lura Media, San Diego, 1993. ("Clay was my teacher, and from the clay process I have drawn a model for change...I am speaking of internal change that results in a new form and shape in the physical world. That is the heart of this book: conscious, embodied change." p. 15)

BARTHOLOMEW, MARTHA, **Tellers of Story, Keepers of Dreams.** Wyndham hall Press, Bristol IN. (The story of "The Potter's Jar," retold from Tales of Tasaqibona.)

Behrensohn, Paulus, **Finding One's Way with Clay**, Simon and Schuster, New York, 1972.This book may well be a pioneer in the field of craft books, combining "how to" with human growth. We learn not only to follow the nature of the clay, but to lead it...we can be thankful because (the instruction) is given in behalf of each of us finding our own way, finding an experience of ourselves that feels real with the help of this responsive and magical material, clay—and that rigorous companion to the art of pottery, the fire. To 'FIND ONE'S WAY WITH CLAY' is to integrate one's inner search with one's outer practice. {Mary C Richards, In the introduction to the book by Paulus Behrenson., p.11}) "It is important to bring together the technique and the person because the technique by itself tends to lead to dead ends. It comes alive through a person, when it is from a living source." (P.B. in the introduction to his book, **Finding One's Way with Clay**, p. 11.)

BUENING, SISTER HELEN, OSB, *"Woman of Earth: Transformation in Clay and Fire"* in **Benedictines1983. (**Referred to in text as HELEN OF ATCHISON, as she has given unlimited permission to quote her and use her materials).

CAMPBELL, PETER A. and MCMAHON, EDWIN M. **Biospirituality: Focusing as a Way to Grow,** Loyola University Press, 3441 North Ashland Ave. Chicago, IL, 1985. This book was the beginning of a close relationship with Jane Cors Smith, my co-worker at St. Vincent Church in Elkhart, In. She brought the book to me one day and asked me to read it because she wanted 'to learn to focus.' We found the focusing process and the process of praying with clay very similar, supportive of one another, and we benefited greatly from the insight.

CAPACCHIONE, LUCIA, **Recovery of Your Inner Child.** Simon and Schuster, New York, 1991(I used this book not only for my own recovery work but also in working with several groups of other adult children of alcoholics who wanted to work on their recovery issues in company with others.)

CLEMMONS, WM. P. **Discovering the Depths.** Broadman, Nashville, 1976. (Guided meditations designed to lead you along a journey into deeper dimensions of spiritual living.)

DeMELLO, ANTHONY, **Sadhana: A way to God**. Image Books by Doubleday, Poona, India, 1984. (Exercise 46: "Living Flame of Love," used with Puja Lamp Prayer.)

_____ **Wellsprings**. Doubleday, Garden City, N.Y. 1985

FARRELL, EDWARD J. **Surprised by the Spirit**. Dimensions, Denville, N.J. 1973. (Extensive use of meditations starting on p. 115 and extending to p 125.)

FRANCK, FREDERICK. **The Zen of Seeing: Seeing/Drawing as Meditation**. Vintage Books of Random House, New York, 1973. (This book, and others by Frederick Franck have served as building blocks in the foundation for my work in meditation with clay.)

_____. **Messenger of the Heart: the Book of Angelus Silesius**. Crossroad, New York, 1982. (Contains translations of Angelus Silesius' writings and observations from ancient masters. The 17th century European mystical poet's verses form a bridge between the spirituality of the East and the West. Quotations used with permission of Frederick Franck.)

GENDLIN, EUGENE, **Focusing**. Bantam, New Age Books. New York, 1979. Gives the psychological underpinnings of the process of focusing which I learned from Pete Campbell and Ed McMahon.

GREEN, THOMAS H. **When the Well Runs Dry**. Ave Maria Press, Notre Dame, IN, 1979. (Part two, Chapter four, 'The Potter's Clay," pp 97 to 119 led me to the passage from Jeremiah in which God sends Israel to the Potter during a period of dryness in prayer.)

HALPIN, MARLENE, O.P. **Imagine That!** Wm. C. Brown, Dubuque, 1982 (Another building block book in my development, this time in the use of the imagination in prayer.)

_____ Puddles of Knowing. Wm. C. Brown, Dubuque, 1984. (Helping children to pray by using their imagination.)

HARRIS, MARIA. **Dance of the Spirit: Seven Steps of Women's Spirituality**, Bantam Books. New York, 1989. (Maria includes references to praying with clay, especially on pp.67 and 68, and a process to follow, called *'Molding your Spirituality,'* on p. 82.)

HAWKINS, THOMAS R. **The Potter and the Clay: Meditations on Spiritual Growth**. The Upper Room, Nashville. 1986. (Image of the potter and the clay are metaphors used effectively in this book to explore Christian spiritual formation.)

HAYS, EDWARD, **Prayers for the Domestic Church**. Forest of Peace Books, Inc. Easton, KS, 1979. (With permission, I used the prayer, *'Blessed are Your, Lord our God, Who Has Filled Creation with Light and Splendor,'* p. 52 in the Puja LAMP experience.)

JONES, ALEXANDER, Gen. Ed., **The Jerusalem Bible**, Doubleday and Co. Garden City, N.Y. 1996.

KEYES, MARGARET FRINGS. **Inward Journey: Art as Therapy**. Open Court Publishing Co., LaSalle IL, 1992. (I have used 'Family Sculpture,' pp 21-33 with recovery groups.)

McMAHON, EDWIN. **Beyond the Myth of Dominance, An Alternative to a Violent Society**. Sheed and Ward, Kansas City, MO, Shows how intimacy with oneself is the key to intimacy with others. The ways men and women react differently to intimacy is examined with special attention given to the dominant spirituality of our day; the spirituality of control.

RUPP, JOYCE, **Dear Heart, Come Home: the Path of Midlife Spirituality**. Crossroad. New York, 1996. Joyce uses guided imagery, rituals and chants in guiding the reader on the inward journey.

SIMA, JOHN ROSS, S.J. **Clay Speaks to us of God: Images from Peru for Our Daily Prayer**. Centro de Espiritualdidad Ignaciana, Lima, Peru, 1996. (The author, a missionary in Peru, attempts to take a path close to personal experience, that of actually working with clay, and relating it to the spiritual life. The author proposes reaching some very concrete goals, deepening the contemplation of some Biblical texts from the experience of working with clay and understanding the relationship between people and their God through the use of images of clay in the Bible.)

TICKERHOOF, BERNIE, T.O.T.S.F. "How to Pray with Your Imagination." In PRAYING Magazine # 31. July-August, 1989, pp. 5-7.(I have used ideas from this article in explaining the Imaging in prayer process.)

UNSWORTH, JEAN MORMON. "**Sharing the Crucifixion**," PRAYING MAGAZINE #83 March 1, 1998, pp 4-8. Published by National Catholic Reporter, Kansas City, MO.(This article inspired me to take my clay with me to Mary's Solitude at St. Mary's Notre Dame for the triduum of Holy Week, 1998. See Holy Week pp 46-50)

VON FRANZ, MARIA, **Interpretation of Fairytales**, Ch VII, p. 6 in 1970 edition…Spring Publications, NY. (See Bird of Paradise imaging, p. 44)

WEIDERKEHR, MACRINA, OSB, **Seasons of Your Heart: Prayers and Reflections on Faith, Mystery, Love, Hope, Wonder**. Harper, San Francisco, 1979. (Macrina uses guided imagery in many of her books. This one has a section on "Earthen Vessels," pp 49-51.Also a reflection on 'Love is not Blind'. I Cor. 13: 4-7 on pages 64-76.)

Marianne McGriffin, S.P.

TOPICAL INDEX

ABOUT THE AUTHOR

Sister Marianne McGriffin is a Sister of Providence of St.-Mary-of-the-Woods, Indiana. She taught school for twenty-five years, and served as Director of Religious Education in parishes for seventeen years before entering into her third career of Spiritual Direction and Consultant in Religious Formation.

Founder and Director of **Open Spaces**, in Elkhart Indiana for over thirteen years, Sister Marianne has worked in spiritual formation and led activities such as personal growth groups, retreats and spiritual direction.

She is highly qualified educationally as well as experientially, having studied and interned in focusing and spirituality with Peter Campbell and Ed McMahon of the Institute for Research in Spirituality, and is certified with the Shalem Institute in Spiritual Formation, Washington, DC.

Printed in the United States
1175500001B/210-343